Children's Games
from Around
the World

About the Author

Dr. Glenn Kirchner is an internationally recognized expert in elementary school physical education. His teaching career includes elementary school through university teacher education programs. He has travelled to many countries as an expert clinician and visiting professor. As an author, he has an impressive list of books, manuals, and articles. His textbook *Physical Education for Elementary School Children* is now in its seventh edition and is considered a leading text in elementary school physical education. Dr. Kirchner has also produced and/or directed over thirty instructional films which have been widely distributed throughout the world.

Children's Games from Around the World

Glenn Kirchner

Wm. C. Brown Publishers

Cover design by John R. Rokusek

Illustrations by Diane M. Smith

Copyright © 1991 by Wm. C. Brown Publishers. All rights reserved

Library of Congress Catalog Card Number: 89–85882

ISBN 0–697–11738–3

Printed in the United States of America by Wm. C. Brown Publishers, 2460 Kerper Boulevard, Dubuque, IA 52001

10 9 8 7 6 5 4 3 2 1

Contents

Preface

A few years ago, I started an International Games Project which was designed to collect three different types of games from around the world. The first, called Traditional Games, are the running, tag, manipulative, and simple team games children have played since recorded history. The second type, known as Inventive or Creative Games, are the result of a child's response to a teacher's verbal challenge. In this form of activity, the teacher sets the limitations within which children use their creative talents to make up their own games. The third type, known as Cooperative Games, is very similar to the second as the teacher sets the limitations relating to such factors as number of players and equipment. However, in addition to this, these games must possess one or more cooperative elements, such as equality, participation, or trust.

An instructional package describing the way each of the different types of games was to be documented, along with a request for accompanying photographs and children's drawings of their games, was sent to teachers, colleagues, and friends throughout the world. By the end of the first year, I received over four hundred games from thirteen countries. Many of these games were accompanied by photographs of the children playing their traditional and newly created games. In addition, several teachers sent collections of drawings made by the children to illustrate how their game was played. The success of that first year's collection prompted me to extend the project for another two years to gain a wider geographical and cultural sampling. The project ended in 1987 with over seven hundred games from twenty-six countries representing all continents.

As I began to edit each game, I tried to keep it as close to the original version as possible. However, there were games where I had to add a rule, change a sentence, or even change the title to cope with different meanings of words and phrases. While some of the photographs that were submitted are excellent, others may appear a little out of focus or not quite up to professional standards. This is because they were taken by the teachers who may not have had much photographic experience. Nevertheless, it was felt they should be included so that teachers and children from other countries would have a visual idea of where these games came from. As almost all of the children's drawings were done in crayon or watercolor, the black and white copies in this book do not do justice to their artistic talents. However, they do provide a very pleasant impression of how these young artists felt about their games. Finally, there are eighty-seven computer generated illustrations that are used to clarify the boundaries and general flavor of the games.

When the participating teachers sent their games to me they often added a note about the projects and how their students reacted to making up their own games. They noticed a positive change in the children as they began to invent their own games, particularly those of a cooperative nature. This was one of the reasons the teachers gave for planning to continue to use this new approach in their program. If the reader also feels there is merit in the creative and cooperative games approach, he or she will be interested in Part Four which provides a step by step procedure for introducing this approach to elementary school-age children.

Acknowledgments

There are numerous colleagues and friends who provided me with many contacts throughout the world. Although I cannot acknowledge all of them by name, they have my thanks for all those introductory letters.

The computer generated illustrations provided in each chapter were created by Diane M. Smith. Her illustrations not only help clarify the rules and regulations of each game, but also capture the fun and excitement of the games.

I would like to give special thanks to my wife for her creative ideas and thorough editing.

The following list of names represents directors of physical education, college teachers, supervisors, and teachers—all of whom gave so generously to this book. To each of them my sincere appreciation. Without their efforts and the creative responses of their students, this book would never have been written.

Argentina
Professor L. A. Izarduy, Director of National Physical Education and Sports; Mr. M. A. Rezzano, teacher; Mrs. A. L. Virue de Caracciolo, teacher.

Australia
Mr. B. Churchward, Lecturer, Mount Lawley Campus, Western Australia; Mr. F. Wood, teacher; Mr. J. Woodward, teacher; Ms. M. Wincup, Lecturer, School of Physical Education, Underdale Site, South Australia; Mrs. D. A. Monceau, teacher; Ms. D. Peake, teacher; Mrs. J. Best, teacher.

Barbados
Ms. A. Brathwaite, teacher; Ms. G. Bailey, teacher; Mr. M. Stoote, teacher; Ms. B. Howard, teacher.

Belgium
Professor R. Renson, Institute of Physical Education, Leuven; Mr. B. Eeclhode, teacher; Mr. C. Schaartz, teacher; Ms. A. Kooreman, teacher; Ms. A. Verreth, teacher; Ms. S. Van Laere, teacher; Professor W. Porte, Hoger Institout Voor Lichamelijke Opvoeding; Dr. D. Van Wouve, Lecturer; Dr. H. Smulders, Lecturer; Dr. B. Vanreusel, Lecturer.

Botswana

Mrs. V. Macdonald, Education Officer, North Kanye; Mrs. M. Mbikiwa, teacher; Mr. L. B. Bogusing, teacher.

Canada

Mr. T. Kikcio, Program Consultant, Saskatoon, Saskatchewan; Mr. D. Bates, teacher; Mr. D. Wipf, teacher; Mr. J. Borland, teacher; Mr. B. McKay, Gabriel Dumont Institute, Regina, Saskatchewan; Mr. G. Smith, Physical Education Supervisor, McCreary, Manitoba; Mr. F. Clark, teacher; Mr. B. Gooden, teacher; Mr. B. Brinksworth, teacher; Mr. F. Hanley, Consultant, Department of Education, Fredericton, New Brunswick; Mr. D. Wilson, teacher; Mrs. D. Tait, teacher; Mr. E. M. Kulmatycki, Coordinator, Red Deer, Alberta; Mr. Stevensen, teacher; Mr. B. Wotherspoon, teacher; Mr. M. Villeneuve, teacher; Mrs. S. Plumber, teacher; Mrs. M. Isenor, teacher; Mr. B. Farnham, teacher.

China

Ms. G. Shou, teacher, Shanghai Elementary School, Shanghai, China.

England

Mr. C. Cox, Senior Advisor for Physical Education, Chester; Mr. G. Firth, teacher; Mr. J. Oliver, teacher; Mr. C. Pritchard, teacher; Mrs. G. Garnett, teacher; Mr. C. M. Gill, teacher; Mrs. H. Madeley, teacher; Mrs. I. G. Metcalf, teacher; Ms. A. C. Thompson, teacher; Mrs. M. Jameson, teacher; Mrs. P. Cunningham, teacher; Mr. K. N. Jones, teacher.

France

Madame S. Martine, Institute d'ecole Primaire Francais; Jaunay Clan, teacher; Mr. F. Dart, teacher.

Germany

Professor W. D. Brettschneider, Universitat Gesamthochschule, Paderborn; Professor J. Kretchmer, Universitat Hamberg; Ms. Hans-Joachim Schnabel, teacher; Professor D. Brodtman, Universitat Hannover.

Greece

Mr. P. Konstantinakos, Coordinator, General Secretary of Sport, Athens; Mr. N. Nikitaras, teacher.

Holland

Mr. P. C. Limburg, Director, Research Institute, Arnhem; Ms. T. Steen, teacher; Mr. G. Burken, teacher.

India
Dr. N. Radhakrishnan, University of Baroda; Ms. Swati Jain, teacher; Ms. R. Singh, teacher; Mr. A. H. Goradia, teacher.

Italy
Dre. E. Ricatti, Ministere Della Publica Instrruzione; Professor A. Berini; Mr. G. Frisa, teacher; Ms. Gividici, teacher; Mr. B. Feltri, teacher; Mr. G. Guidici, teacher.

Jamaica
Ms. K. Simpson, Education Officer, Ministry of Education, Kingston; Mr. D. Smith, teacher; Ms. C. Wilson, teacher.

Japan
Mr. Y. Matsumoto, Instructor, Kyushu Otani College; Mrs. M. Haesgawa, teacher.

Luxembourg
Mr. R. Decker, Institut Superieur D'Etudes Et De Recherches Pedago-gigées; Ms. A. Marc, teacher; Mr. W. Nico, teacher.

Malawi
Mrs. H. Carle, teacher, Mzimba; Mrs. M. Nhlema, teacher.

New Zealand
Ms. J. Silver, Senior Adviser on Physical Education, Department of Education, Auckland; Mr. K. Hornby, teacher; Mr. D. Douche, teacher; Ms. R. Denly, teacher.

Peru
Professors L. Matos and F. Temoche, Universidad Nacional De Trujillo; Mr. R. Segura, General Director, Continuing Education; Mr. F. N. Rodriguez, Director, Physical Education and Sports.

Scotland
Mrs. I. R. Drummond, Head Teacher, Helensburgh, Dunhartonshire; Ms. J. Howie, teacher.

South Africa
Mrs. J. E. Du Toit, Lecturer, Department of Physical Education, Universiteit Van Stellenbosch; Ms. J. A. Skibbe, teacher; Mrs. M. C. Grant, teacher; Ms. L. Hutcheson, teacher; Ms. L. Rbeeder, teacher; Mrs. M. Levvennick, teacher.

Sweden

Mr. S. T. Andersson, Lecturer, Stockholm Institute of Education; Mr. B. Lundquist, teacher; Mr. K. van Malmburg, teacher.

Thailand

Mr. S. Puangbootr, Director General, Department of Physical Education, National Stadium, Bangkok, Thailand.

United States

Mrs. M. Reimer, teacher; Ms. D. Long, teacher; Ms. N. Hovde, teacher; Mr. R. Metz, teacher; Mr. G. Brown, teacher; Ms. L. Vitaglione, teacher; Mr. R. Rhatigan, teacher; Mr. R. Marston, Professor, University of Northern Iowa; Mr. V. Else, teacher; Ms. K. Needham, teacher; Ms. J. Barnes, teacher; Ms. N. Schreiber, teacher.

Wales

Mrs. A. Lyons, teacher, St. Clare's Convent Prep School, Porthcawl, Mid Glam, South Wales.

Introduction

In 1823 Alfonso X, the Spanish king of Castile, compiled one of the first game books in recorded history. Since then many other books have been written about the various types of games played by children, youth, and adults. Some of these publications, such as Joseph Strutt's *Sports and Pastimes of the People of England,* written in 1898, and Edward and Elizabeth Lucas's book, *Three Hundred Games and Pastimes,* published in 1900, are collections of games with historical background about how, why, and where the games were played. Contemporary books on this topic often provide theories as to why children play particular types of games along with descriptions of games played in various parts of the world.

This book, a result of a three year collaborative project conducted with hundreds of elementary school teachers from twenty-six participating countries, is different from the above publications in that, as well as traditional games, it also includes new games that the children from these countries have discovered for themselves. In Part One, the traditional games that have been played for centuries are described and illustrated. Many of these games are also accompanied by photographs and drawings which were done by the children themselves.

Part Two contains a variety of new games that were created by children. These games were arrived at through a process in which their teachers posed special challenges that required one or more players to make up games using a variety of inexpensive equipment such as balls, sticks, and other small objects. A selection of the games contained in this part of the book are also accompanied by children's drawings or by photographs.

Part Three is an extension of the new games section. It contains cooperative games that were designed by the children using the same process of posing special challenges with an important criterion added. Each challenge in Part Three required the game to include one or more elements of cooperative behavior. These elements were defined as equality, participation, success, and trust. Like the two previous sections, these new cooperative games are generously illustrated with drawings and photographs.

The initial intent of this book was to provide a reservoir of old and new games for the participating teachers to share. The traditional games of Part One clearly illustrate the common purpose games had in the past and will continue to have in the future for children of all ages regardless of their cultural backgrounds. It is hoped the new games in Parts Two and Three will be played by other children and then added to their own reservoir of enjoyable games. It is the wish of the teachers and children who participated in this project that this will be the case and that their contributions, particularly those games of a cooperative nature, will in this way provide a closer bond of understanding and friendship between all nations.

Part One

Traditional Games

Part One contains over seventy traditional games played by children in every part of the world. These are not the highly organized sports like basketball and soccer; rather, they are the uncomplicated games that require little equipment and are played in the streets, vacant lots, or parks by city kids and in the open fields and forests by country kids. They include running games which generally involve one or more taggers, boundaries, and special rules. They also include simple ball games and guessing and manipulative games like marbles, hopscotch, and rock, scissors, paper.

One of the most interesting features of these traditional games is that they are all, with one or two exceptions, competitive in nature. A single player either competes against another player, as in hopscotch or marbles, or as part of a team against another group. Children are either tagged, caught, or in some way eliminated from the game until a winner is declared. An interesting discovery of this project was that participating teachers and children honestly believed that their contribution, be it "Kick the Can," "Prisoner's Base," or "Drop the Hanky," was unique to their country. They could not believe their game was played by other children from different cultural backgrounds and geographical locations around the world. What we find is quite the contrary; the various types of traditional games, described and illustrated in Part One, are the universal language of children. These games, as you will soon read, may have different names and slight variations in the rules, but they are played by children of all ages and in most countries of the world. A few examples of these "universal" games are provided under each type of traditional game.

As adults, we present numerous theories as to why children play these games. For the young player, the rationale may not go beyond one very important reason—to enjoy the excitement of the game.

1

Running and Tag Games

The games included in this section are perhaps the oldest and most well-known games played by children in every country. They normally involve a lot of running, dodging, and especially tagging one another.

Running and Tag Games

Running and Tag Games

1   Kick the Can

Country: Canada
Type: Tag
Players: Class
Age: 8–12
Equipment: 1 tin can

FIGURE 1.1   . . . if the player gets to the can first . . .

How to Play

One player is chosen to be "It" and stands in a circle next to a tin can. When "It" closes her eyes and begins to count aloud to fifty, all other players run and hide. After "It" counts to fifty, she begins to look for hidden players. When she finds a player they both run for the tin can. If "It" tags the can first she says, "one, two, three," and the name of the player. Then that player goes to a designated "Jail." However, if the player gets to the can first, he/ she kicks the can as far as possible to release any player(s) in jail. "It" must replace the can and count to fifty before she starts looking for hidden players again. The game continues until all players are caught or "It" is changed after a set period of time.

Variations:

- India: "Esha Desai" (I Spy). In India, the game is played in a similar fashion except, to start the game, any player picks up the tin can and throws it under her leg as far as possible. Once "It" returns the can to the circle, all she has to do is visually "spot" a player who becomes the new "It."

FIGURE 1.2   . . . and throws it under her leg.

- Holland: "Burkuit" (Kick the Can). A favorite street game and played exactly the same as the Canadian version—except children hide in and around buildings.

- Sweden: "Paven Bann-lyser" (The Pope). In Sweden, "The Pope" stands on a small hill, counts to 100 while others run and hide. "The Pope" then goes to find the children. When a child is seen, "The Pope" says: "Peter (the player's name), you are banished." Peter must walk to "The Pope's Hill" and wait until he receives a "wave" (signal) from one of the hidden children. When Peter has been waved free in this way, he must sneak away without being seen by "The Pope." If "The Pope"

"Påven Bannlyser" (The Pope)

FIGURE 1.3   . . . and counts 1–2–3–4.

sees Peter or any other player sneaking away, he or she is banished again. The game continues until a player is banished three times. When this occurs all players come out of hiding and the game begins again with a new Pope.

• Japan: "Kankai." The class is divided into "Taggers" and "Runners." One runner kicks the can out of the circle. As soon as any player on the "Taggers" team returns the can to the circle, all taggers try to tag the runners. When a runner is touched he

FIGURE 1.4   . . . kicks the can . . .

must stand in the circle. However, like the other versions, if a runner can kick the can without being touched, he releases all other runners.

2   Black Cat

Country: Germany

Type: Tag

Players: Class

Age: 8–10

Equipment: Class set of
   skipping ropes

FIGURE 1.5   "Who's afraid of the Black Cat?"

How to Play

One player, "Black Cat," stands on the side of the playing field. The other players, "Mice," stand on the opposite side. Each mouse has a tail (skipping rope tucked into back of shorts). The "Black Cat" calls, "Who's afraid of the Black Cat?" The mice reply "Nobody!" The "Black Cat" says, "I'm coming!" The mice try to run to the opposite side without allowing the cat to step on their tails. When a mouse loses his tail he becomes the "Black Cat" and the game starts over.

3   Snow White

Country: Australia
Type: Tag
Players: Class
Age: 7–12
Equipment: 8 hoops and
    2 cones

FIGURE 1.6   Children who
are tagged go to "The
Dungeon."

How to Play

Children are divided into seven teams. Each team chooses a name of one
of the Seven Dwarfs, such as Happy, Dopey, or Doc. One child is selected
to be "The Witch" (tagger), another child becomes "Snow White" and
stands in the single hoop as shown in the illustration.

All teams line up behind a home line with "The Witch" standing anywhere within the playing area (suitable for indoors as well as outdoors).
"The Witch" calls a name such as "Grumpies" and they try to run to the
opposite line and back before being tagged by "The Witch." The only safe
area is behind the home line. Children who are tagged are sent to "The
Dungeon" (hoops) where they wait to be freed by "Snow White" who can,
at any time, sneak across and touch them to set them free. This is a very
heroic gesture on Snow White's part as she runs the risk of being tagged
by "The Witch." If this happens "Snow White" is replaced by another child.
The game ends when all groups have had a turn at running down and past
"The Witch." A new "Witch" is chosen to restart the next game.

4   Running Steps

Country: South Africa
Type: Tag
Players: 6–20
Age: 9–12
Equipment: Stairs

FIGURE 1.7   "Aar Speler"

FIGURE 1.8   . . . at the bottom of the stairs and calls . . .

FIGURE 1.9   . . . and must move to the step that was called out.

FIGURE 1.10   If "The Caller" calls, "Saturday!" . . .

How to Play

The game can be modified according to the number of steps that are available. Each step is assigned a day of the week. "The Caller" stands on the flat surface at the bottom of the stairs (Saturday) and calls out the name of a day. The players stand on the neutral area at the top of the stairs and must move to the step that was called out. If they move to the wrong step, they are eliminated. If "The Caller" says, "Saturday!" all the players must touch the bottom area with one foot, then run back to neutral area. "The Caller" tries to tag a player as soon as she touches Saturday. However, "The Caller" is not permitted to climb the stairs in pursuit of the players. If a player is tagged she becomes the new "Caller."

5   Scamper Out

Country: Australia

Type: Tag

Players: Class

Age: 8–10

Equipment: 2 hoops, 2
   skittles, and 1 nerf ball

FIGURE 1.11   . . . two "Runners" move forward and attempt to knock . . .

How to Play

Divide class into two teams. Team A are "Runners" and stand in pairs behind the end line. Team B are "Taggers" and may stand anywhere in the playing area. Give the nerf ball to a "Tagger" and place one skittle (bowling pin) in each hoop. "Taggers" may not run with the ball nor hold it longer than three seconds. They may, however, pass the ball to other teammates or run anywhere they wish providing they are not in possession of the ball. On signal from the teacher, two "Runners" move forward and attempt to knock the skittles over, then return home without being tagged (below the waist) by the ball. If the skittle is knocked down before a "Runner" is tagged, his team is awarded one point. If he makes it home without being tagged, his team is awarded an additional point. Each pair on Team A has a turn before the teams exchange positions and "The Taggers" become "The Runners" and try to SCAMPER OUT.

6   Tradhok (Treehawk)

Country: Sweden
Type: Tag
Players: Class
Age: 7–12
Equipment: Designated
  locations marked by items,
  such as trees, traffic cones,
  or beanbags

FIGURE 1.12   "The Hawk"
must find a free tree . . .

How to Play

One player is chosen to be "The Hawk." All other players must find a "tree" (any designated spot) and touch it. The object of the game is for any two players to signal to each other by blinking their eyes then running to each others tree. "The Hawk" must find a free tree before any set of players can complete their exchange. If "The Hawk" is successful, the player who did not reach his tree becomes the new "Hawk" and must call out, "I am the new HAWK," and the game continues.

7   Dog and Bone (Steal the Bacon)

Country: Barbados
Type: Tag
Players: 10–30
Age: 7–12
Equipment: Small item—
  stick, beanbag, etc.

FIGURE 1.13   When a
player picks up "The
Bone" . . .

How to Play

Two teams line up behind their own end line. Each player has a number and the beanbag is placed in the middle of the playing area. The teacher calls out a number, such as four, and "The Fours" from each team race for "The Bone." When a player picks up "The Bone," he must run back across his own end line without being tagged by the opposing number four player. If touched by the opposing player before reaching his end line, his opponent receives one point. On the other hand, if the player reaches his end line without being tagged, his team is awarded one point.

Variations:

- Belgium: "Tie Robbery." Played exactly the same way except that they use a cloth for "The Bone" and call it a "Tie."

- India: "Dog and Bone." This game is played like the two previous countries with one exception. When a number is called, a player must pick up "The Bone" within a specified time—say ten to fifteen seconds. If neither team picks up "The Bone," they return to their own lines and another number is called.

FIGURE 1.14   When a number is called . . .

- Peru: "Struggling Flags." This game is very similar to DOG AND BONE but with a nice variation. Two teams are numbered and stand on a line facing the teacher who is holding a flag in each hand. The teacher calls a number, such as "Five," then these two players race for their flag, run

FIGURE 1.15   . . . two players race for their flag . . .

around their own team, return the flag, and run back to their starting position. The player who returns to his own place first wins one point for his team.

8   Rabbit in the Hole (Squirrel in the Tree)

Country: Peru
Type: Tag
Players: Class
Age: 6–8
Equipment: None

FIGURE 1.16   "The Rabbit" stands in the middle.

FIGURE 1.17   . . . "Rabbit to its hole!" . . .

How to Play

The class is arranged into groups of three, scattered in the playing area. Within each group two players join hands to form a hollow tree and the third player, "The Rabbit," stands in the middle. One of the groups is designated as extra Rabbits which are randomly located in the playing area. When the teacher calls, "Rabbit to its hole!" the two players forming the hole raise their arms to let out "The Rabbit" who, in turn, must run and find a new hole. The extra Rabbits also run to any open hole but only one Rabbit is allowed per hole. The game continues, changing positions between the hole players and "The Rabbits," until all players have had a chance to be a Rabbit.

Note: This game is also played in Australia, Canada, United States, and England usually by the name SQUIRREL IN THE TREE.

9   Moto Kumapiri (Fire on the Mountain)

Country: Malawi
Type: Running
Players: Class
Age: 6–9
Equipment: None

FIGURE 1.18   Suddenly
"It" calls, "Wazima!" . . .

How to Play

One child is chosen to be "It" and the remainder of the class is divided into two groups of the same number. They then form a double circle and face counterclockwise with "It" standing ouside the circle, also facing counterclockwise. "It" begins to run around the circle and sings "Moto kumapiri, moto kumapiri." All players join in the singing "Moto . . . , moto . . ." and both circles begin to run counterclockwise. Suddenly "It" calls "Wazima!" which means the fire is out. When this happens "It" and all the children on the outside circle try to find and hold onto a player on the inside circle. The player who remains alone becomes the new "It" and the game starts over.

10   Stuck in the Mud

Country: England
Type: Tag
Players: Class
Age: 7–12
Equipment: None

FIGURE 1.19   When an
untagged player crawls
under . . .

How to Play

Two or three players are chosen to be "Taggers" with the rest of the class scattered in the playing area. "Taggers" try to tag the other players. When a player is tagged, she must stand with legs apart. When an untagged player crawls under the tagged players legs, she is freed and can join the game again. However, if a player is caught three times she becomes one of "The Taggers." If the turnover is not frequent enough, it would be a good idea to change Taggers every few minutes.

Variations:

- Australia: Same name, same rules.
- Canada: Same name, same rules.
- Germany: "Bridge Tag." Same rules.
- United States: "Smurf Tag." This version is similar to STUCK IN THE MUD with a few space-age additions. "The Tag-

FIGURE 1.20 Bridge Tag

gers" are known as "Gargomels" and are identified by wearing colored pinnies and carrying a nerf ball. All other players are "Smurfs." When a "Smurf" is tagged he must freeze with hands held high and legs apart. He may be released by another "Smurf" crawling through his legs. However, if a "Smurf" is tagged while in the act of crawling through another Smurf's legs, he must stand in front of the would-be liberated "Smurf" with legs apart and hands held high. Both captured "Smurfs" can only be released if another Smurf crawls through both players legs.

Note: This game was designed by children in Brooklyn, New York as a cooperative game. However, since it was so close to STUCK IN THE MUD, it was placed in this section.

11   Cat and Rat

Country: Barbados
Type: Tag
Players: 10–12
Age: 6–8
Equipment: None

FIGURE 1.21   . . . and stands in the middle of the circle.

How to Play

One player is chosen to be "The Rat" and stands in the middle of the circle. Another player is "The Cat" and stands outside the circle which is made up of the remaining players. Circle players hold hands while "Cat" and "Rat" act out the following challenge.

Cat: "I am the Cat."

Rat: "I am the Rat."

Cat: "I can catch you!"

Rat: "No, you can't!"

Chasing game begins after the word "can't." "Rat" and "Cat" may move in and out of the circle by crawling under the joined hands of the circle players. As soon as "The Cat" touches "The Rat," two new players are chosen and the game continues.

Variations:

- Canada: Same name, same game.
- United States: "Cat and Mouse." Circle players join hands and try to prevent "The Cat" from catching "The Mouse" by moving their arms up and down.

12   Somersault

Country: Greece
Type: Running
Players: 20–30
Age: 9–12
Equipment: Long rope

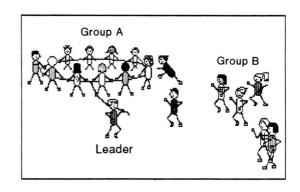

FIGURE 1.22   One player ("Leader") of group A holds one end . . .

How to Play

Arrange two teams as shown in the diagram. Children in group A form a circle and hold on to the rope with both hands. One player ("Leader") of group A holds one end of the rope. Players from group B try to jump on the backs of group A. The Leader of group A is allowed to move around the circle while holding the end of the rope, to try and stop group B players from climbing onto the backs of his teammates. The Leader of group A cannot use his hands . . . only the rope or his body to hinder "The Attacker." If a player successfully climbs onto a group A player's back, the "A" player must carry him to a designated line. Player A remains behind the line and Player B returns to the game. The aim is for players from group B to climb onto the back of each player in group A, thus eliminating them from the game. Rotate positions and repeat game.

13   Red Rover

Country: United States
Type: Tag
Players: Class
Age: 7–12
Equipment: None

FIGURE 1.23   . . . "Red Rover, if you don't come I'll . . ."

How to Play

One player is chosen to be "The Tagger" and stands halfway between the goal line and another line at the opposite end of the playing area. All other players stand behind one goal line. The game starts when "The Tagger" calls, "Red Rover, if you don't come I'll pull away!" After this call, all of the players try to run across to the opposite goal without being tagged. All of those tagged join "The Tagger" and help to tag the rest when the original "Tagger" gives the call again. The game continues until all players are caught. The last one caught becomes "The Tagger" for the next game.

This game can be played with the following variation: After "The Tagger" has caught four to five players, the runners on the goal line have two choices. They may continue to try to run to safety or they may stay behind the line to "tug." To "tug," the people on the goal line call out, "Tug!" and then take the first hand offered them by one of "The Taggers." If the person on the goal line can pull the tagged person over the line she has a free run to the other line. If the person on the goal line is pulled over by the tagged player, he becomes a tagged player.

Variations:

- England: "British Bull-dog." Instead of each player being tagged, "It" has to catch a "Runner" and hold him off the ground while he says, "British Bull Dog one-two-three." If "The Tagger" can hold the player off the ground for the count, that player becomes another tagger. If "The Tagger" cannot hold "The Runner" off the ground for the required count, the runner is freed and continues to run to the opposite line.

FIGURE 1.24   . . . and continues to run to the . . .

- South Africa: "Open Gates." Same rules as the United States.

- New Zealand: "Bull Rush." The game begins with "It" calling out the name of one player who must then run the length of the playing area without being tagged. If the runner is caught he helps "The Tagger" and another player is called

FIGURE 1.25   Same rules as the United States.

to run. If the runner is successful in reaching the goal line, all other players can run together to the line. The game continues until every player is tagged.

- Canada: "Pom Pom Pull Away." Same rules as the United States. As well as an indoor game, this game is also played in rural areas on skates on outdoor rinks where the call is, "Pom, Pom Pull Away. If you don't come, we'll drag you away!"

- "Octopus." In this other Canadian variation of the traditional game, two or three players are chosen to be "It." The remaining players line up on the end of the playing area. To begin, the "Its" yell "Octopus!" This signals the players to try to run to the opposite safety zone without being tagged. Any tagged players must stand at the spot where they were tagged. Again, when the "Its" yell "Octopus!" the untagged players try to move to the opposite safety zone. This time, however, the runners must be more wary because in addition to the mobile taggers, the "frozen" tagged players may pivot on the spot and tag them. The game continues until there are two or three players remaining untagged. These players become the "Its" for the next game.

14   Old Eagle

Country: China
Type: Tag
Players: 10–12
Age: 6–8
Equipment: None

FIGURE 1.26 "The Chicks" hold each other's shoulders . . .

How to Play

One player is chosen to be "The Old Eagle," another is "The Chicken," and the remaining players are "Chicks." The "Chicks" hold each others shoulders and hide behind the mother Chicken, who tries to keep between "The Old Eagle" and her Chicks. "The Old Eagle" tries to tag any Chick. When a Chick is caught he must sit down on the side and wait until the last Chick is caught.

15   S-T-O-P, Comma, Comma, Full Stop

Country: Scotland
Type: Running
Players: 5–15
Age: 6–8
Equipment: None

FIGURE 1.27   . . . and keeps on running while the other players sing . . .

How to Play

The game starts with all players standing in a line one behind the other, facing the same direction. The first player runs forward and keeps on running while the other players sing, "S-T-O-P, Comma, Comma, Full Stop." When they say (instead of spell) "Stop," the runner must stop and stand still. Then, the next player in line repeats the same action. When the second player stops, she and the runner before her try to touch each other. If they can touch without moving their feet, they run to the back of the line. If they cannot touch, the next person in line runs and stops and tries to touch one of the players before him.

16   Ice Cream (Red Light)

Country: Wales
Type: Running
Players: Class
Age: 6–8
Equipment: None

FIGURE 1.28   . . . she quickly turns around . . .

How to Play

One player is chosen to be "It" and faces the wall. All other players stand on a line about thirty feet away. "It" begins to spell aloud, "I-C-E-C-R-E-A-M." When she finishes spelling the word, she quickly turns around to catch anyone moving forward. When a player is caught she must stand next to "It" and place one hand on the wall while all other players return to the starting line. The game starts again, and if anyone can get to the wall before "It" finishes spelling the word, the caught players are freed and all runners head back to the starting line. "It" runs after them and if she tags one, that player becomes the new "It." If not, she remains "It" and the game continues.

Variations:

- Canada: "Red Light." Same rules, same game.
- Jamaica: "Red Light." Same game except that "It" counts one to ten, and says "Red Light" before turning around to catch the players who are still moving.
- United States: "Red Light." Same as Jamaica.
- Sweden: "Sneaking." Same rules. "It" counts one to five and turns around quickly.

FIGURE 1.29   Same rules, same game.

- Peru: "One-Two-Three O'clock." One person is "It" and faces away from the other players who start on a line about twenty-five feet away. When "It" calls out "One-Two-Three," all players can walk forward. As soon as "It" says "O'clock!" he quickly turns around to catch any player still moving. Any player who is caught moving even slightly,

FIGURE 1.30 . . . he quickly turns around . . .

must stand motionless on the spot where he was caught. The game continues with remaining active players. As soon as one of these players makes it all the way to the line, touches "It," and says "One-Two-Three O'clock," they change positions and the game starts over.

17   Drop the Hanky

Country: China
Type: Running
Players: Class
Age: 1–12
Equipment: Piece of cloth

FIGURE 1.31 . . . sitting in circle formation . . .

How to Play

Arrange six to fifteen players, sitting in circle formation and facing toward the center. Next, one player is chosen to be "It" and is given the piece of cloth as the hanky. "It" walks around the outside of the circle while the others sing and clap their hands. After a few moments "It" drops the hanky behind a player and continues around the circle. If the seated player realizes the hanky has been dropped behind him, he picks up the cloth and chases "It" around the circle. If "It" gets to the player's place before the player, she takes his place in the circle and the player becomes "It." However, if "It" is tagged before reaching the empty space she is given the hanky again and continues to be "It." Another situation results if the seated player does not realize the hanky has been dropped behind him. If this is the case, "It" runs around the circle then picks up the cloth still laying behind the seated player and hits him with it. These players then exchange positions and the game continues.

Variations:

- England: Same name, same rules.
- Thailand: "Mon Son Pha." Same rules.
- Luxembourg: Same name, same rules.
- Italy: "Il Gioco Del Cĕrchio" (Circle Game). One child is placed in the center of the circle to clap her hands quickly or slowly. The "It" player must move around the outside of the circle in time to the rhythm of the clapping. When the center player stops clapping, the outside player must touch the shoulder of the nearest child seated in the circle. The game continues as above.
- France: "La Chandelle" (The Candle). The game is similar to the one played in China with a few changes in the rules. "It" is called "The Mailman." "The Mailman" drops the hanky behind a player and says, "The Mailman has come." If "The Mailman" can run around the circle and back to the empty space without being tagged, the other player becomes the new Mailman and the game goes on as before. However, if the player with the cloth touches "The Mailman"

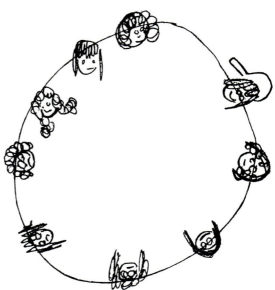

FIGURE 1.32   "It" is called "The Mailman."

before he reaches the empty space, "The Mailman" goes to the center of the circle. While he is standing in the center, the other children sing:

"Close the little peas

The Mailman has not come

He will come tomorrow morning

One o'clock, two o'clock, . . . sing to twelve o'clock."

After the rhyme, the "Old Mailman" takes the player's position and the tagged player becomes the "New Mailman."

18   Stinger

Country: South Africa

Type: Tag

Players: Class

Age: 8–12

Equipment: Utility ball and a
   traffic cone

FIGURE 1.33   Any player
throws the ball at the
cone . . .

How to Play

In a designated playing area players form a circle with their legs apart.
A traffic cone or similar object is placed in the center of the circle. Any
player throws the ball at the cone and tries to hit it; if he misses he tries
again. The ball then rolls off the traffic cone toward any player. The player
who is touched by the ball is "It" and he then picks up the ball. When he
does so, the other players are allowed to move anywhere within the designated playing area while "It" counts aloud to ten. At the count of ten all
players must stop moving. "It" throws the ball at any player attempting to
hit him below the waist. The players may use their fists to prevent the ball
from touching their bodies but if the ball does touch any other part of their
bodies, they become "It" 's helpers. Once this happens, the player with
the ball is no longer allowed to run with it. He may throw it at a free player
or to another "It" player in order to get a better throwing position. The
game ends when all players have been hit.

19   Lemon, Lemon

Country: Belgium

Type: Running

Players: 10–12

Age: 7–10

Equipment: Chairs

FIGURE 1.34   . . . each
pair sitting directly across
from . . .

How to Play

Players are arranged in pairs and each pair is given the name of a fruit, other than lemon. The players sit on chairs in a circle formation with each pair sitting directly across from each other on opposite sides of the circle. One player is chosen to be "It" and stands in the middle. When "It" shouts one, two, or three fruit names, these players have to exchange places with their partner. During the exchange, "It" tries to sit down on one of the chairs before the player gets to it. This leaves one person without a chair and he becomes the new "It." When the middle player shouts "Lemon, Lemon!" *all* the players have to exchange places with their partners.

20   Prisoner's Base

Country: Many countries
Type: Tag
Players: Class
Age: 8–12
Equipment: None

FIGURE 1.35   . . . having a base (home) . . .

We usually think the games we played as children were not very old and were probably passed on to us after originating with our parents or grade school teachers. To end this section on running and tag games, let's look at a very popular game currently played in many countries throughout the world. We will start with a little history of the game and see what happened to it over a few hundred years.

One of the earliest recordings of Prisoner's Base was during the reign of Edward III (1327–77). In those days it was known as "Base" or "Prisoner's Bar." Adults played the following version on the grounds of Westminister Palace with such exuberance that it interfered with parliamentary affairs and was banned by Edward III.

How to Play

"The performance of this pastime requires two parties of equal number, each of them having a base or home, as it is usually called, to themselves, at the distance of about twenty yards. The players then, on either side, take hold of hands and extend themselves in length, opposite to each other, as far as they conveniently can, always remembering that one of them must touch the base. When any one of them quits the hand of his fellow and runs into the field, which is called giving the chase, he is immediately followed by one of his opponents; he again is followed by a second from the former side, and he by a second opponent; and so on alternately, until as many are out as choose to run. Everyone pursues the man he first followed, and no other; and if he overtakes him near enough to touch him, his party claims one point toward their game and both return home. They run forth again and again in like manner, until the number is completed that decides the victory. This number is optional, and I am told rarely exceeds twenty. It is to be observed that every person on either side who touches another during the chase, claims one point for his party, and when many are out, it frequently happens that many are touched.''*

In a delightful book titled ''Three Hundred Games and Pastimes,'' written in 1903, the game became known as CHEVY or PRISONER'S BASE and with slight variations, it is still played in the following manner.

FIGURE 1.36   ''Chevy''

''The game is started by one player (A1 = Bill) running out of his camp and calling ''CHEVY.'' As soon as Bill leaves Team A's camp, Jim (B1) calls out Bill's name and tries to tag him. The object of each Team A player is to get back to camp before his chaser from Team B can tag him, or to lure his chaser closer to Team A's camp. This is important because as soon as Jim, from Team B, starts to chase Bill, from Team A, another player from Team A, Mary (A2), can call out, run after, and tag Jim from Team B. A player from either team can only chase one player.

''If a player is caught, he goes to his opponent's prison. As soon as a player, for example Bill from Team A, is in Player B's prison he calls out, ''Rescue!'' When this happens, a player from Player A's camp calls ''Prisoner!'' and runs out to rescue him. As soon as this happens, a player from Team B's camp calls out the rescuer's name and tries to tag him before he reaches B's prison. If the rescuer is tagged he becomes another prisoner. If he reaches the prison first, both members from team A are given free passage back to their camp.''

---

*Strutt, J., *The Sports and Pastimes of the People of England,* London, Chatto and Windus, 1898.

2

Ball Games

These games are an example of the worldwide influence contemporary team sports have upon young children. Most of the following games involve an inflated ball that is either thrown, bounced, or kicked. They require skills similar to those of the major team sports and use modified playing areas and rules to meet the level of interest and ability of the younger child.

Ball Games

1   Seven Sins

Country: Peru
Type: Ball
Players: 9–12
Age: 8–12
Equipment: Utility ball

FIGURE 2.1   Player number one throws the ball into the air . . .

How to Play

Player number one stands in the middle of a circle formed by the remaining players. All other players are numbered from two upwards. Player number one throws the ball into the air and simultaneously calls out the number of one of the circle players. As soon as a number, for example "Two," is called, all other players run away from the circle. When number two catches the ball, he calls out "Stop!" and everyone must remain motionless. Player number two may now take three steps toward the nearest child and throw the ball at him. If that player is hit, he is charged with one sin. The game starts over and continues in this fashion until a player has been hit seven times (Seven Sins). When this occurs he is required to perform something, such as make a funny face or say a rhyme, and then change places with player number one.

Variation:

- England: "Three Bad Eggs." One player is chosen to be "It" and stands in the middle of the circle with a ball (tennis or utility ball). The rest of the players each pick the name of a color or make of car, etc. Then one member of the team calls out the selected colors to the person who is it. "It" throws the ball in the air and shouts out one of the colors, for example "Red," and the player with this color runs to get the ball. While she runs to get the ball the remaining team players run off to other parts of the playground, and keep running until "It" shouts "Stop!" Then the players must stop and stand still with their legs apart while the person with the ball tries to throw it between the legs of the nearest player. If the ball goes through his legs, that standing player gets ONE BAD EGG. When one of the players gets THREE BAD EGGS he becomes "It."

2   Brunt

Country: Germany
Type: Ball
Players: 12–20
Age: 8–12
Equipment: 1 ball, 4 traffic
   cones, and 1 hoop

FIGURE 2.2   The first player of team A throws or kicks . . .

How to Play

Arrange two teams as shown in the drawing. The first player of team A throws or kicks the ball into the playing area and starts to run around the four markers. The markers can be traffic cones or gymnastic apparatus, such as vaulting horses, which the children like because of the next rule. The running player may stop at or on any marker and wait for the next throw by her teammate. Two or more players may wait at any marker. When a ball is thrown, players from team B try to catch it, then run and place it in the hoop and call out "BRUNT!" If any player on team A is caught off any marker at the moment "Brunt" is called, the teams change positions. One point is awarded for each completed trip around the four markers.

3   Borden Ball

Country: Canada
Type: Ball
Players: Class
Age: 9–12
Equipment: 1 inflated ball

FIGURE 2.3   The ball may be thrown in any direction . . .

How to Play

Place one goalie from each team in an eight-foot goal area in the center of each line (use two posts or traffic cones as goalposts). The object is to throw the ball through the opponent's goal. The game begins with a jump ball between two opposing players at the centerline. The ball may be thrown in any direction, but it may not be hit or kicked. A player may take a maximum of three steps and cannot hold the ball longer than three seconds. On penalties the ball is given to the nearest opponent. Members of the team that do not have possession of the ball may check the player with the ball, but they may not touch, hold, or push him. One point is awarded for each goal. After a point is scored, at halftime, or at any official stopping of play, restart play with a jump ball at the center. If the ball goes over the sidelines, a player on the opposing team throws it into the field of play.

4   Open Ball

Country: New Zealand
Type: Ball
Players: Class
Age: 10–12
Equipment: 1 ball, 2 goals
(traffic cones)

FIGURE 2.4   . . . players may also run with the ball until they are tagged . . .

How to Play

The class is divided into two equal teams. The aim of the game is for each team to get the ball through their opponent's unmanned goal. The starting team, selected by a jump ball, may pass the ball by hitting it with their hands or kicking it with their feet. These players may also run with the ball until they are tagged by the opposing team. When this happens they must immediately, and without looking, throw it backwards over their head. The team that catches the ball resumes the play toward their opponent's goal. If any player catches a kicked ball before it bounces she gets a free throw or kick at the goal. One point is awarded for each goal and the team with the highest number of points wins the game.

5   Four Goal Soccer

Country: Peru

Type: Ball

Players: 10–16

Age: 8–12

Equipment: 4 goals and a
    soccer ball

FIGURE 2.5   . . . each team attacks and defends two goals.

How to Play

The playing area is bounded by four lines. Place four goals (traffic cones or sticks) in the center of each line. Team A's goals are on the North and West side of the field. Team B's are on the East and South side. The game is played without goalies and each team attacks and defends two goals. Soccer rules apply with the exception of the offside and corner kick rules.

6   Dodgeball

Country: United States

Type: Ball

Players: 20–30

Age: 8–12

Equipment: 1 utility ball

How to Play

One team forms a large circle, and the other team stands in the center of it. On signal, circle players try to hit inside players below the waist with the ball. To avoid being hit, the inside players may move anywhere within the circle. Outside players may enter the circle to retrieve the ball; however, they may not throw at an opponent while inside the circle. Any player hit below the waist joins the outside circle. The last person remaining in the circle is the winner. Add two more balls according to the playing ability of the class.

Variations:

• Barbados: "Dog and Geese Dodgeball." In this variation, the team in the center holds on to the waist of the player in front to form a chain. The object is for the circle players to hit the last player in the chain. All center team members must keep contact with each other and protect the end player from being hit. When the end player is hit, teams change positions and the game continues.

FIGURE 2.6   . . . object is for circle players to hit the last player . . .

• Luxembourg: "Rectangular Dodgeball." The teams face off in rectangular courts as shown in the illustration. Each team tries to hit the opposing team below the

FIGURE 2.7   . . . he moves behind Team B's court . . .

waist. When a player on Team A is hit, he moves behind Team B's court and if he gets the ball he continues to try and hit Team B players. The same applies for Team B players. The game ends when all players of either team are removed from their courts.

• Jamaica: "Dandy Shandy." Divide the class into two equal teams and toss a coin to decide which team will be in the bordered area first ("The Dodgers"). The other team spreads around the bordered area to retrieve balls for the two players chosen to be "Throwers." Two or more balls can be used. The "Throwers" stand opposite each other and

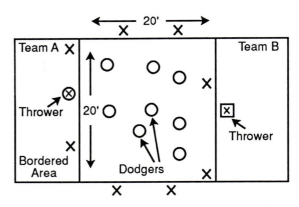

FIGURE 2.8   "Dandy Shandy"

try to hit players inside the area with the balls. Any player hit with a ball is required to stand outside the bordered area and join the throwers team as a retriever. After all players are hit the other team goes inside the bordered area, and the game is repeated. If the last player from any team dodges ten consecutive balls, her team is allowed to return to the bordered area and dodge balls again.

• Peru: "Matagente" (Killers). The players are arranged as shown in the diagram. The two outside players, "The Killers," throw from behind the end line and try to hit other players below the waist. "Killers" may retrieve the ball from inside or outside the designated playing area but must return to their end line before throwing the ball. Inside players may move anywhere in the rectangular area. If a player is hit, the first time he loses his skin, the second time

FIGURE 2.9   . . . "Killers" try to hit . . .

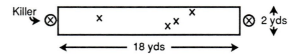

FIGURE 2.10   "Matagente"

he loses one life, and the third time he is out of the game. If an inside player can catch a ball before it touches the ground, he gains one life. This player can keep this "spare" life or give it to another player who may have to leave the game.

7   Calcio Seduto (Crab Soccer)

Country: Italy

Type: Ball

Players: Class

Age: 8–12

Equipment: 1 ball and
    2 goals

FIGURE 2.11   . . . players
are always on all fours . . .

How to Play

Arrange the playing area as shown in the illustration. The rules are the same as regular soccer, with the goal posts (three by two yards) but without the goal and out of bound areas. The players are always on all fours in a crab walk position (balancing on the hands and feet with the back to the floor). Only the goalies can guard or touch the ball with their hands. The other players can only use their feet or heads to move the ball.

Variation:

• Peru: "Futbol de Toros." This version is similar to the above game with a few enjoyable variations. Players begin in a crab walk position and may move the ball with hands, feet, or head. When the whistle blows, players turn over and must move on hands and feet. When the ball goes out of the circle, any opponent may retrieve it and bring it back to the place where it went out, and continue the game. Any time the whistle blows means a change in playing positions.

8   Kitchen Ball

Country: Botswana

Type: Ball

Players: Class

Age: 7–10

Equipment: 1 ball for each
    team

FIGURE 2.12   . . . the ball
is passed . . .

FIGURE 2.13   "How to Play"

How to Play

Each team stands in a line with their feet apart. Player number one on each team holds the ball about chest high. On the signal, "Go," the ball is passed through their legs to the end player. The end player takes the ball to the front of the team and repeats the action. The team that finishes first wins the relay.

9   The Fly

Country: France
Type: Ball
Players: 5–6
Age: 8–12
Equipment: 1 ball

FIGURE 2.14   . . . with their hands clasped together.

How to Play

One player is designated as "The Leader" and holds the ball while all other players stand on a line with their hands clasped together. "The Leader" then throws the ball to one of the players who must try to catch it, throw it back, and immediately reclasp the hands. After two or three throws, "The Leader" begins to fake throws in order to tempt any player to release her hands in order to catch the ball. Every fair catch receives one "fly" and any player who opens her hands incorrectly is deducted one "fly." The player who gets to ten flies first changes positions with "The Leader."

10   Beat the Ball

Country: England
Type: Ball
Players: 6–12 on each team
Age: 7–12
Equipment: 1 small ball

FIGURE 2.15   The bowler throws the ball and the batter . . .

How to Play

Two teams are arranged as shown in the illustration. Four players on the fielding team form a stationary rectangle; the other players scatter in the playing area. The bowler throws the ball and the batter tries to hit it with his hand into the playing area, then run around the four stationary players. Any poorly thrown ball is rethrown. If the batter can run around all four players in the rectangle before the fielding team can field the ball and throw it to player one and sequentially around to player four, he scores one point. Each batter has a turn, then teams change positions.

11   Ulu Maika (Rolling Stone Disks)

Country: United States
  (Hawaii)
Type: Ball
Players: Class
Age: 7–12
Equipment: Softball or
  similar sized utility balls

FIGURE 2.16   . . . or roll
them through . . .

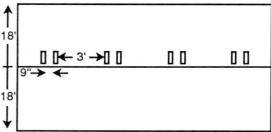

FIGURE 2.17   Ulu Maika

How to Play

"Ulu Maika" or "Olohu" was played in early Hawaii with rounded stones called "ulu." Men used to either roll the stones as far as they could to show their strength or roll them through stakes to demonstrate their accuracy in bowling.

Arrange players on opposite lines facing the two stakes. Each player tries to roll the ball through the two stakes. One point is scored for each time the ball rolls through the stakes without knocking them down. Game continues to a predetermined number such as eleven, fifteen, or twenty-one points. This game may be played with two players or as a team event involving two or more players on each team.

Variation:

• "Ihe Pahee" (Spear Sliding). This is actually another similar game called Ihe Pahee or Spear Sliding. The spear should be about five feet long (perhaps old broom handles) and rounded at each end. The game is played with the same rules as Ulu Maika except that each player tries to slide his spear through the stakes. Keep all players at least eighteen feet away from the stakes and not directly in line with the two stakes.

FIGURE 2.18   . . . slide his spear through the stakes.

12   Aranga Touch

Country: New Zealand
Type: Ball
Players: Class
Age: 10–12
Equipment: 1 ball, 2 goals

FIGURE 2.19   Players may run with or pass . . .

How to Play

Arrange the playing area as shown in the illustration. Two players from each team are appointed to be "The Defender" and "The Catcher." The game is started by a pass from the center. Players may run with or pass the ball anywhere within the playing area. The team without the ball gains possession by intercepting a ball or tagging an opponent who has the ball. When a player with the ball is tagged he must give it to "The Tagger." One point is scored if the catcher catches the ball on the fly.

A player kicking the ball or contacting an opponent, other than by a tag, must stand on the sideline until a point is scored. When a ball is thrown or carried out-of-bounds, the team that did not commit the error gets a throw-in at the spot where the ball went out-of-bounds. Both "Catchers" and "Defenders" must stay behind the end lines. If "The Catcher" drops a pass, no point is scored and "The Defender" takes possession. Following a point, the game is restarted by the non-scoring team from the center circle.

3

Manipulative and Guessing Games

Manipulative and guessing games include a very broad and diverse collection of activities. Most of the games in this chapter, such as Gummi Twist, Marbles, and Hopscotch, involve manipulating part of the body or an object in a particular way.

Manipulative and Guessing Games

1   Gummi Twist

Country: Germany

Type: Manipulative

Players: 3–4 per set

Age: 8–12

Equipment: Elastic band
    approximately nine feet
    long, end's tied. Use leg
    sections of panty hose as a
    substitute elastic band.

FIGURE 3.1   . . . performs
a series of jumping . . .

How to Play

Two players stand inside the stretched elastic band. The band is around their ankles on the first round. The first player performs a series of jumping steps moving in and out of the banded area. Each player who follows must imitate all movements performed by the first player. If any player makes a mistake, he is replaced by the next player. When the first player takes his turn again (second round), the band is raised to knee high and the player may repeat her movements or create a new series of movements for each player to imitate.

Variations from other countries include: (1) changing the height to hip, armpits, and neck, (2) performing routines that include jumping on one foot and touching the hand with the other foot, and (3) performing routines with a partner or while holding a piece of equipment.

Other Countries Playing This Game:

• Argentina: Elastic Band. Same rules.

• Holland: Elastic Twist. Same rules.

• Peru: Laliga. Same rules.

• South Africa: Goommy. Same rules.

FIGURE 3.2   . . . in South
Africa . . .

FIGURE 3.3
. . . in Peru . . .

2 Telegram

Country: Belgium
Type: Guessing
Players: 6–15
Age: 7–12
Equipment: None

FIGURE 3.4   . . . "I'm
sending a telegram to
Mary". . .

How to Play

One player is chosen to be "It" and stands in the middle of the circle as shown in the illustration. Circle players stand and hold hands. One player in the circle says, "I'm sending a telegram to Mary" (the name of a circle player), presses the hand on her right or left side, and calls out, "Started." The player who receives the pressed signal passes it on to the next circle player. This continues until it arrives at Mary, who says, "Arrived!" The center player tries to intercept the telegram by watching, and if he sees a person pressing the next player's hand, he says his/her name. If the center player is correct, he changes positions with the circle player.

3   We Are from Tlhahana

Country: Botswana
Type: Manipulative
Players: Class
Age: 8–10
Equipment: 1 small stone or
object per player

FIGURE 3.5   . . . each player quickly places his stone . . .

FIGURE 3.6   "We are from . . ."

How to Play

Children sit in a circle and hold a small stone in their right hand. They sing the song while holding onto their stone. When they sing the chorus, each player quickly places his stone on the ground in front of the player on his right. Each player tries to pick up the next stone as quickly as possible and place it in front of the person on his right side. Only one stone may be picked up at a time. The object is to try not to have any stones in front of you when the chorus ends.

Song

We are from tlha ba ne.
[Re tswa kwa tlha ha ne]

We are selling the goods.
[Re ba pa tsa di lo]

Repeat two lines.

Chorus

Do you want to sell the goods?
[A o rata go re ki sa]

Do you want to bury them?
[A o rata go re - ka]

4   Rocky Boat

Country: Japan
Type: Manipulative
Players: 7–8 per team
Age: 10–12
Equipment: None

FIGURE 3.7   . . . player on Team B jumps . . .

How to Play

Arrange class into two equal teams. Player one of Team A leans against the wall and player two places his arms around player one's waist. All other players on Team A do the same. The first player on Team B jumps on the back of the last player and tries to move forward. Team A cannot attempt to force any player from Team B off their backs. However, if a player on Team B touches the floor after jumping onto Team A, he must return to his starting position and not move forward until the last player on his team has had his turn. Teams change positions and the team with the most players remaining on top wins the game.

5   Queenie I.O.

Country: England
Type: Manipulating and
   guessing
Players: 5–7
Age: 6–9
Equipment: Small object

FIGURE 3.8   . . . throws
the ball backward over . . .

How to Play

Player A throws the ball backward over her head in the direction of other players. After throwing the ball, player A remains facing away from them. When the ball has been caught and hidden away, usually in their hands behind their back, they begin to chant:

"Queenie I.O.

Who's got the ball I.O.?

It isn't in my pocket

It isn't between my legs

Hop Scotch" (They hop from one foot to the other).

When chanting begins, A turns around to guess who has the ball. To further this aim, A may ask each player to turn around, which they must do, carefully hiding the ball if they have it, or pretending to hide it if they haven't. Player A may also run through the group. If she does, the other players also turn around to conceal the ball as she passes through the group. After A runs through the group, she must make a guess. If she guesses correctly, another turn is taken. If not, the person who has successfully concealed the ball takes A's place.

6 Marbles

Country: Canada
Type: Manipulative
Players: 2–6
Age: 7–12
Equipment: Marbles

FIGURE 3.9 . . . most popular and enduring games . . .

Marbles has been one of the most popular and enduring games in the world. There is evidence the game was played in ancient Egypt and pre-Christian Roman times. Each country has its own variation of the game and uses different terms to describe playing positions, rules, and the marbles themselves. English children say "taws" while Americans use terms such as "steelies," "jumbos," and "peewees" to describe the variety of different sized marbles they use in their game. The following games, sent from four continents, illustrate the fun and excitement children reap from the many variations of this activity.

How to Play

A circle about one foot in diameter is drawn on the ground and each player puts two or three marbles inside the circle. A second outer circle about six feet in diameter is drawn around the circle. The playing order is determined by each player throwing his shooting marble toward a line or wall six to ten feet away. The player whose marble is closest to the line shoots first; the player whose marble is next closest shoots after him, and so on. A player takes his first shot from anywhere outside the circle and attempts to knock the marbles out of the inner circle. If he knocks one or more marbles out of the inner circle, he wins them and takes another shot from where his marble came to rest. If he fails to knock a marble out of the inner circle, his turns ends and he must leave his shooting marble where it stopped. The next player takes his turn and may shoot at any marble within either circle. Whenever a player's shooting marble hits another player's shooting marble, the latter must give him one marble. After all players have had a turn, the first player shoots from where his marble last came to rest. The game ends when all marbles have been cleared from the inner circle.

Variations:

• Luxembourg:
"Smashers." The first player rolls his marble into a designated playing area (square or circle). Each succeeding player tries to hit any player's marble in the playing area. If successful, he keeps it and continues. If a player lost his marble in the previous round, he must start with his second marble from outside the playing area. Play continues until one player has won all the marbles.

FIGURE 3.10   . . . to hit any player's marble . . .

• Japan: "Five Hole Marbles." The playing area has five small holes as shown in the diagram. Player number one shoots from beside hole one and tries to roll his marble into hole two. If successful, the marble remains in the hole. The second player takes his turn and if he hits player number one's marble, providing it is not in the hole, player one is out of the game. Player two takes another turn. If player two's marble goes into the hole, player three takes his turn and the game continues until one of the players returns to hole number one.

FIGURE 3.11   If a player two's marble . . .

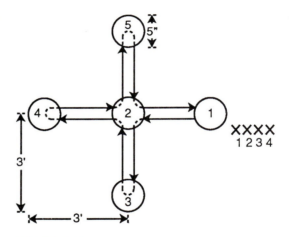

FIGURE 3.12

• Peru: "Road Runner." A pathway is drawn on any flat surface. Each player tries to roll his marble as far as he can without it going out-of-bounds. If it goes over the boundary lines, he is out of the game. The next player takes his turn and, if he hits another player's marble sitting in the pathway and knocks it out-of-bounds, that player is out of the game and the shooting player is given another turn. The first player to reach the finish line wins the game.

FIGURE 3.13   . . . tries to roll his marble as far . . .

7   Kambabi

Country: Malawi

Type: Manipulative

Players: 2–4

Age: 8–12

Equipment: 1 large marble
  and 16 to 20 small marbles

FIGURE 3.14   A handful of
marbles are thrown . . .

How to Play

Players sit around a scooped out hole which is about two feet in diameter. A handful of marbles (or small stones) are thrown into the hole by player number one. Next, she throws a large marble or stone into the air and, before she catches it, must push all of the marbles out of the hole. From here, she must throw the stone into the air again and push one marble back into the hole before she catches the stone. She continues returning them, one at a time, until the last marble has been pushed into the hole. After the last marble is pushed into the hole, she throws the stone up and pushes all the marbles out again. The game continues with her returning the marbles to the hole, two at a time, with each throw. This is followed by "threes," and so on until all are returned with one push. If player number one makes a mistake during any part of this game, the next player is given her turn.

8   Klinkslagen (Cat)

Country: Belgium

Type: Manipulative

Players: 2 per game

Age: 10–12

Equipment: 1 short stick and
  1 long stick

FIGURE 3.15   The batsman
tries to hit . . .

Diagram of Playing Area, Equipment, and Positions

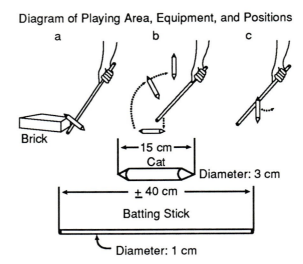

FIGURE 3.16

How to Play

"The Cat" (small stick) is placed against the brick (or a piece of wood) in such a way that the batsman can put the batting stick under "The Cat" in order to hurl it away (see diagram). Immediately after "The Cat" is lifted and hit (B + C), the batting stick is dropped on the ground. The second player has to try to catch "The Cat" in the air. If "The Cat" is caught, then the batsman is out and the playing roles are reversed. If the catcher cannot catch "The Cat," he has to throw it from the place where it landed and try to hit the batting stick where it was dropped by the batsman. If the batting stick is hit, the batsman is out and the playing roles are reversed.

If the second player doesn't hit the batting stick, the batsman gets three chances to hurl and hit "The Cat" as far as possible. The latter is done as follows: on the place where "The Cat" landed, the batsman tries to hit "The Cat" with the batting stick on the pointed end in such a way that "The Cat" rises in the air (see diagram B). While "The Cat" rises in the air, the player tries to hit it a second time to send it as far as possible (see diagram C). Measure the distance from the first hit to the landing position of the third hit. Now the playing roles are reversed and the second player repeats the above procedure. Measure the second player's distance. The longest distance wins the game.

9 Giischt

Country: Luxembourg

Type: Manipulative

Players: 2–4

Age: 8–12

Equipment: 1 short stick 10
cm and 1 long stick 35 cm

FIGURE 3.17 Player B
attempts to throw the
"giischt" . . .

FIGURE 3.18 . . . player
A, using his long stick . . .

How to Play

Player A with the long stick defends a two foot square goal next to the wall. Player B holds the small stick (giischt) and stands behind a throwing line about ten feet away. Player B attempts to throw his "giischt" into the small square. Player A tries to touch the "giischt" with his long stick before it lands in the goal or if the "giischt" falls somewhere outside of the goal area, he is awarded three hits at the "giischt." A hit is performed by hitting the end of his long stick on the sharp end of the "giischt" to cause it to hop up. As the "giischt" is in the air, player A tries to hit it as far as possible. After two more hits, player A, using his long stick as a unit of measurement, measures the distance between the "giischt" and the goal area. Each player takes his turn and the winner is the one who has the highest score.

10   Hopscotch

Country: United States
Type: Manipulative
Players: 2–4
Age: 7–12
Equipment: Small objects
    such as beads or buttons

FIGURE 3.19   . . . one of
the oldest games . . .

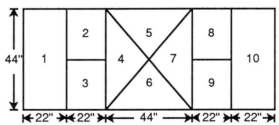

FIGURE 3.20   American
Hopscotch

Hopscotch is one of the oldest known games that children have played in nearly every part of the world. Although no one knows its origin, credit can be given to soldiers of the Roman Empire for teaching the game to children throughout Europe and Asia Minor. Throughout the centuries, each country added new versions, however, as illustrated, the game is still played in much the same way.

How to Play

The first player stands on her right foot (this is her declared "hopping" foot and must be used throughout her turn), outside area one, holding the "puck" (beanbag, button, etc.) in her hand. She tosses the puck into area one, hops into this area, picks up the puck while balancing on her right leg, then hops out. She next throws the puck into area two, hops back into area one, and then moves into areas two and three placing one foot in each area, straddling the two areas. In this position she picks up the puck, hops into area two and then out, hopping through area one to do so. She continues this pattern, hopping and landing with one foot in single spaces and with both feet in adjacent areas. Two hops are permitted in area ten in order to turn around. A player is out if she steps on a line, tosses the puck onto a line or into the wrong area, changes feet on single hops, or touches her hand or other foot during any hopping or retrieving movement. When a child commits an error, she goes to the back of the line.

Variations:

- France: "Hopscotch." The game follows the same basic rules of American hopscotch with the player hopping on one foot in single squares and landing with both feet in adjacent squares. However, when a player lands with one foot in area seven and the other in area eight, he must jump up, turn around in the air, and land in the same areas.

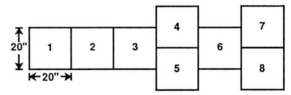

FIGURE 3.21   French Hopscotch

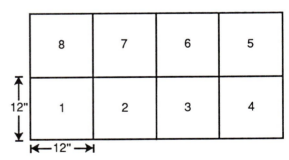

FIGURE 3.22   Italian Hopscotch

- Italy: "Hopscotch." The first player stands on one foot outside square one, holding a "puck" (beanbag, etc.) in his hand. He throws the puck into square one and then hops into this area. Still standing on one foot, he kicks the puck into square two, then hops into that square. He continues this pattern to square eight. When he reaches square eight, he places both feet on the ground, picks up "the puck," and hops backwards through all squares to the starting position. A player is out if he steps on a line, if his "puck" stops on a line, if he puts both feet down in any square except eight, or if he changes feet. When a child commits an error, he goes to the back of the line.

• Holland: "Hopscotch" (Heaven and Earth Hopscotch).

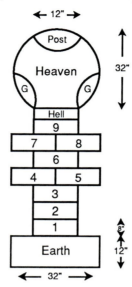

FIGURE 3.23 Dutch Hopscotch

Step 1: The first player stands on one foot inside the "Earth" square holding "the puck" in her hand. She throws the puck into square one, hops to square one, picks up "the puck," and hops back to "Earth." She throws "the puck" to square two, hops to square two, picks up "the puck" and throws it back to "Earth," then hops back to "Earth." Continue same pattern to square nine. Starting from "Earth," throw the puck into "Heaven," and if it lands there, hop to "Heaven," pick up "the puck," throw it to nine, and follow the same procedure back to "Earth." If "the puck" lands in area "Post," a player may not speak or laugh during her turn. If this rule is violated, a player loses her turn. If "the puck" lands in area "Hell," the player loses her turn and must start from the beginning when she takes her next turn. If the puck lands in area six, a player may skip any one of the following steps:

Step 2: Instead of throwing "the puck," kick it from square to square with your foot.

Step 3: Balance "the puck" on your head as you hop through all squares.

Step 4: Begin in the "Earth" square but facing the opposite direction. Throw the puck over your shoulder and if "the puck" lands inside any square, it may be used throughout the game as a "safe house." You can rest in this square on both feet and other players must skip this square during their turn.

If a player makes a mistake during any part of the game, her turn ends and the next player begins. When a player starts her second turn, it begins where she made her last mistake.

11   Leap Frog

Country: Scotland
Type: Manipulative
Players: Class
Age: 8–12
Equipment: None

FIGURE 3.24 . . . bend forward, place their hands . . .

How to Play

Arrange the class into lines of six to eight players. All players except the last one bend forward, place their hands on their knees, and keep their heads down. The last player in each line runs forward, places his hands on the player's back, and straddle jumps over him. Once the last player in line has jumped over the player in front of him, the new "last player" stands up and begins his run and jumping action. Game continues until the first player in the line has finished jumping over all players and says, "Stop!" The children may decide to raise the height of the "frogs" or change the distance between each player before starting the next game.

Variations:

- Belgium: "Leap Frog." This game is played according to the same rules as above with one exception. When the last player reaches the front of the line, he may change the direction of the line. The line keeps on this new course until the second to original last player reaches the front of the line, then he can change directions.
- Italy: "Circle Leap Frog." Children arrange themselves in pairs that are equal in terms of relative height and weight. Next, pairs form a double circle with the children on the inner circle assuming the leapfrog position facing toward the center of the circle. Outer players leap over their partners, crawl through their legs, repeat both actions again, then run clockwise around the circle. When they return to their places they jump onto their partner's back and off, and exchange positions. The second partner repeats the actions of his partner. The first player to arrive back to his starting position and onto his partner's back wins the game.

12   Rock, Scissors, Paper

Country: United States
Type: Manipulative
Players: Class
Age: 9–12
Equipment: None

Rock   Scissors   Paper

FIGURE 3.25   Rock,
Scissors, Paper

(clenched
fist)

(hand flat
palm downwards)

How to Play

Children first learn three symbols which are: (1) "Rock"—clenched fist, (2) "Scissors"—two fingers out simulating a pair of scissors, and (3) "Paper"—flat hand, palm facing down. Divide the playing area into two equal halves. Designate a center line and two end lines. Each team first decides which symbol to "Throw" (Rock—Scissors—or Paper), then lines up on opposite sides of the center line. Pecking order is: Rock breaks Scissors, Scissors cut Paper, and Paper covers Rock. When the teacher says "Go!" each team must "throw" their symbols. The chosen symbols are thrown and the team which wins chases their opponents, attempting to tag them before they can cross their end line. A tagged player joins the team which tagged him.

13   Rope Skipping

Country: Wales
Type: Manipulative
Players: 2–20
Age: 6–12
Equipment: Small and large
   ropes

FIGURE 3.26   Rope
Skipping

Rope skipping, whether performed individually, with a partner, or large group is enjoyed by children on every continent. It is, like hopscotch and marbles, a very old pastime with its own vocabulary of movement and age-old rhymes to accompany the various jumping movements.

Variations:

• Barbados: "All in To-
gether Girls." Two
players turn the rope and
the first pair runs in and
skips together. As they
are skipping all other
players sing:

"All in together girls

This is fine weather girls

When it comes to your
birthday

Please jump out."

FIGURE 3.27   All in Together Girls

At the end of the rhyme,
they sing the months of the year. When the month each child was born is called, that player runs out. If either one of the jumpers makes a mistake they exchange positions with the rope turners.

China: "Doubles." Two
children begin standing
side by side with the
rope held in their out-
side hands. As they start
jumping, one player
turns out then back in
followed by his partner
repeating the move-
ment. One player can
also start skipping, then
his partner enters and
holds the waist of the
jumper and both skip to-
gether.

FIGURE 3.28   . . . one turns out then . . .

- Canada: "Group Jumping." Two children start turning a long rope. Other players enter one at a time until ten to twelve players are jumping together. A ball can be added to this game and passed overhead from the front jumper to the next jumper and on to the end of the line.

FIGURE 3.29   . . . until ten to twelve players . . .

14   Easa Matessa

Country: Scotland
Type: Manipulative
Players: 5–10
Age: 7–10
Equipment: None

FIGURE 3.30   . . . player who says number five goes . . .

How to Play

To begin the game all the players stand in a circle. One player is chosen to start. The other players stand with the palms of their hands facing the sky. The game progresses counterclockwise with the starter putting his right hand on the next player's left palm. That person puts her right hand on the next person's left palm, and this continues around the circle. At the same time everyone says a rhyme that goes like this:

"Easa Matessa oh, oh, oh. Crocodile Matessa oh, oh, oh, hello, hello. One, two, three, four, five."

The player who says number five goes into the middle. The game continues until there are only two players left. The person who does not go into the middle is the winner.

Part Two

New Games

The games included in Part Two are those that have been invented by children from each of the participating countries. They are the result of a standardized format all teachers agreed to follow. The procedure required each teacher to pose four specific challenges to his or her class. For example, in the first challenge, the teacher first arranged her class into pairs and gave each a ball and two small pieces of equipment. She then posed the challenge: "Make up a game that has two players, one ball, a throw, a catch, and one goal." Players were then given a few minutes to create and play their new game.

The documentation of each game was done in several ways. In some instances, the teacher described the game while, in others, the children not only described their game but included their own drawings to illustrate how the game was played.

The games that follow are organized according to four challenges the teachers were asked to present to their classes. Chapter 4 involves a challenge designed for two players. Chapters 5 and 6 involve similar challenges for five players and for the whole class. Chapter 7 includes a selection of different challenges made up by the participating teachers.

4

Games Involving Two Players

The challenge described below is the first of four posed to all children who participated in this project. Starting with two rather than one player was done to allow for some initial sharing of ideas between players. In addition, providing only one ball, and specifying the type of skill and number of goals to be used, provided a reasonably easy structure to develop their first new game. The reader will note that children from markedly different cultural backgrounds were equally creative in their approach to this first challenge. However, like their traditional games, there is an ever-present element of competition in each new game.

CHALLENGE: "MAKE UP A GAME THAT HAS TWO PLAYERS, ONE BALL, A THROW, A CATCH, AND ONE GOAL."

Number	Country	Name of Game	Page
1	England	Butterflies	67
2	Japan	Hit the Ball	68
3	Scotland	Throw, Catch, and Run	68
4	Botswana	Bucket Ball	69
5	Australia	Super Duper Hoop	69
6	South Africa	Hop, Skip, and Jump	70
7	Wales	Ball Catch	70
8	Peru	Magazine Ball	71
9	France	Flying Goalie	72
10	Canada	Catch a Falling Star	72
11	Belgium	Skittle Ball	73
12	New Zealand	Trick the Guard	74
13	United States	Scoop Ball	75
14	England	Ball in the Basket	75
15	Canada	Two Person Catch Ball	76
16	Luxembourg	Reaction Ball	76
17	Germany	Hoop Hunting	77

1   Butterflies

Country: England
Type: Ball
Players: 2
Age: 7–8
Equipment: A small ball and
    container

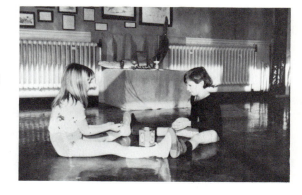

FIGURE 4.1   Player "A"
throws to "B" . . .

How to Play

Two players sit on the floor, legs apart and feet touching. This position gave them the idea for the name, "Butterflies." Player "A" throws to "B" and if "B" catches the ball, she has a chance to throw the ball into the container. If successful, she gets one point. If she fails to catch the ball, she retrieves it then throws it to player "A" who then takes her turn. If a ball is thrown too high or too wide, it is returned to the thrower and re-thrown.

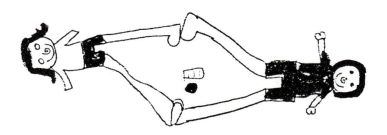

FIGURE 4.2   NUNA, AGE 7

2   Hit the Ball

Country: Japan
Players: 2
Age: 9–12
Equipment: 2 markers and
   2 utility balls

FIGURE 4.3   . . . attempts
to throw the ball . . .

How to Play

Player "A" stands behind the goal with a ball in his hands. Another ball is placed about five feet in front of the goal. Player "B" stands about fifteen feet in front of the goal. Player "A" throws the ball to "B," who tries to catch it. If he fails to catch it, he must run after it and hold the ball where it finally stopped. Player "B" now attempts to throw his ball at the stationary ball located five feet in front of the goal and try to knock it into the goal. If player "B" fails to hit the stationary ball or if it fails to roll into the goal, players change positions. One point is awarded for each successful goal.

3   Throw, Catch, and Run

Country: Scotland
Type: Ball
Players: 2
Age: 8–10
Equipment: Small ball, box,
   and post

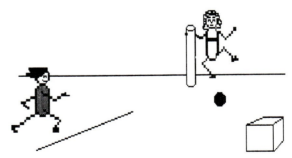

FIGURE 4.4   Player "B"
throws the ball . . .

How to Play

Arrange post, box, and throwing distance according to the children's level of skill. Player "A" must hold on to the post and player "B" holds a ball and stands behind the throwing line. Player "B" throws the ball and if it lands and remains in the box, she gets one point and another try. Player "A" must remain at the post until the ball has landed in the box or on the ground. Player "B" throws the ball again and if it does not land and remain in the box, player "B" must fetch it and return it to the box before player "A" can run around the box and back to the post. If player "A" gets back first, they exchange positions. If player "B" gets back first, she gets another turn.

4   Bucket Ball

Country: Botswana
Type: Ball
Players: 2
Age: 8–12
Equipment: 1 ball and
    1 basket

FIGURE 4.5   Bucket Ball

How to Play

Player "A" stands behind the basket with a ball. Player "B" stands behind the starting line. Player "A" throws the ball to "B," who tries to catch it. Player "B" throws the ball from where she caught or retrieved it, toward the basket. If the ball lands and remains in the basket, she scores one point and gets another turn. If she fails to score a goal, she changes positions with player "A."

5   Super Duper Hoop

Country: Australia
Type: Ball and Tag
Players: 2
Age: 8–12
Equipment: 1 ball and
    3 hoops

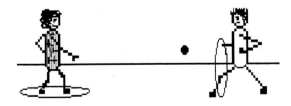

FIGURE 4.6   If the ball
passes through player . . .

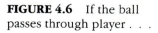

How to Play

Place two hoops on the ground about twelve to fifteen feet apart. Player "A" stands in one hoop and throws the ball to player "B" who holds the other hoop at her side. If the ball passes through player "B" 's hoop, he drops the hoop and runs to home base and back. At the same time, player "A" runs after the ball, picks it up, and tries to hit player "B" below the waist before she can return to her hoop. If player "B" is successful, she is awarded one point and another turn. If unsuccessful, players exchange positions.

6   Hop, Skip, and Jump

Country: South Africa

Type: Throw

Players: 2

Age: 8–12

Equipment: 4 hoops, 4 traffic
  cones, and a ball

FIGURE 4.7   . . . and
throws a ball into . . .

How to Play

Each player has a hoop on the ground and one balancing on top of two traffic cones. Player "A" stands in her own goal and throws a ball into player "B" 's goal, then runs back to her own hoop on the ground. At the same time, player "B" runs from her hoop and attempts to catch the ball on the first rebound out of her goal. If she catches the ball in this manner, she gets one point. Change positions after each throw. If a throw does not land in the hoop area it is retaken by the same player.

7   Ball Catch

Country: Wales

Type: Ball

Players: 2

Age: 8–10

Equipment: 1 small ball and
  1 basket

FIGURE 4.8   If Player "B"
catches it . . .

How to Play

Players stand about three feet on each side of a basket. Player "A" throws the ball to Player "B." If Player "B" catches it she receives one point. Then both players step backwards one step. If a player misses the catch she retrieves the ball, returns to her position, then steps back at the same time as her opponent. Players continue throwing, catching, and stepping backwards until one player has five points. Players do not step backwards after a player has scored five points, however, the next time the player with five points catches a ball, he tries to throw it into the basket. One point is awarded for each ball that touches the basket and five points if it remains in the basket. The ball is returned to this player, who then throws it to the other player, and the game continues until one player has ten points.

8   Magazine Ball

Country: Peru

Type: Ball

Players: 2

Age: 8–12

Equipment: Magazine, a ball,
  and a wastepaper basket

FIGURE 4.9   He tries to throw the ball . . .

How to Play

The first player stands behind a line about six feet away from the basket holding a ball on a magazine. He tries to throw the ball into the basket. If successful, he gets one point and another turn. If the ball fails to remain in the basket, players exchange positions. The first player to get five points wins the game.

9   Flying Goalie

Country: France
Type: Ball
Players: 2
Age: 10–12
Equipment: 1 goal and 1 ball

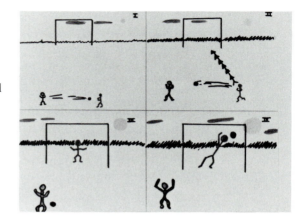

FIGURE 4.10

How to Play

   Two players start about twenty yards away from the goal (I). They begin to dribble and pass the ball back and forth until one player reaches the shooting line (about ten yards from the goal) while he has possession of the ball (II). At this moment, he passes the ball to the other player and rushes to become the goalie (III). The player who receives the ball must try to score a goal before the other player gets into position, or after, by dribbling and attempting to score (IV). One point for each successful goal and the first player to receive five points wins the game.

10   Catch a Falling Star

Country: Canada
Type: Ball
Players: 2
Age: 8–12
Equipment: Ball and small
   target (box or basket)

FIGURE 4.11   Player "A"
stands beside the target . . .

FIGURE 4.12   Catch a
Falling Star

How to Play

Draw or designate a rectangular playing area according to the playing ability of the children. Place a target on one end of the playing area. Player "A" stands beside the target and throws the ball upward so it will land in the designated playing area. If it goes out-of-bounds, it is retaken. Player "B" starts from behind the opposite end of the playing area and tries to catch the ball before it lands in the playing area. If he catches the ball he receives one point and a free throw at the target. If he hits the target, he gets another point and another turn. Player "A" must stand at least three feet away from the target while the free throw is taken. If he misses the catch or the target the players change positions. The first player to score ten points wins the game.

11   Skittle Ball

Country: Belgium
Type: Ball
Players: 2
Age: 10–12
Equipment: 3 traffic cones
    and 1 ball

FIGURE 4.13   Skittle Ball

How to Play

Arrange traffic cones as shown in the drawing. The object of this game is to try and hit the highest cone in such a way that the opponent cannot catch the ball before it hits the ground. If a player throws the ball and misses the target, the other player takes his turn. If a player throws the ball and hits the top traffic cone, and his opponent cannot catch it before it hits the ground, one point is awarded the thrower. However, if the opponent catches the ball no point is awarded and players exchange positions. The player with the highest score at the end of the game is the winner.

12   Trick the Guard

Country: New Zealand
Type: Ball
Players: 2
Age: 9–12
Equipment: 1 ball and 1 goal
  (any small container)

FIGURE 4.14   The "Attacker" dribbles the ball . . .

How to Play

One player is "The Attacker" and the other is "The Defender." "The Attacker" dribbles the ball with her hand within her own half of the playing area, until with a dodge or feinting action to fool the defender, she throws the ball high into the opponent's half. She then runs and tries to catch the ball before it lands on the ground. "The Defender" cannot cross the line but can try to block the throw or intercept it before her opponent can retrieve it. If "The Attacker" catches the ball she is given a free throw at the goal. Each player has five turns before exchanging positions. The winner is the player with the highest number of points at the end of the game.

13   Scoop Ball

Country: United States
Type: Ball
Players: 2
Age: 9–12
Equipment: 1 ball, 2 plastic
  bleach bottles, and
  2 hoops

FIGURE 4.15   . . . remain
in their hoops and pass . . .

How to Play

Two players stand in their hoops which are about eight to ten feet apart. Each player has a "scoop" made from an empty bleach bottle. Players must remain in their hoops and pass and catch the ball with their scoops. As one distance is mastered, change throwing hands or lengthen the distance between the hoops.

14   Ball in the Basket

Country: England
Type: Ball
Players: 2
Age: 6–8:
Equipment: 1 ball and
  1 basket

FIGURE 4.16   If the ball
lands and remains . . .

How to Play

The player behind the basket throws the ball to her partner who is standing on the first throwing line. Mark throwing lines according to level of skill of the children. The partner who catches the ball attempts to throw it into the basket. If the ball lands and remains in the basket, she gets one point and moves back to the next throwing line. The throw is repeated and two points are awarded if it lands and remains in the basket. The game is repeated for lines three and four and points awarded according to each line. After the fourth line, positions are changed and the game continues. The player with the highest number of points wins the game.

15   Two Person Catch Ball

Country: Canada
Type: Ball
Players: 2
Age: 7–10
Equipment: 1 ball

FIGURE 4.17   ''The Shooter'' may take three . . .

How to Play

The object of this game is to hit the target with the ball. The target may be marked on the wall or it may be any object which can be defended by ''The Goalie.'' ''The Shooter'' may take three attempts to score. Regardless of the outcome, the goalie and the shooter reverse roles after the shooter's three tries. The game ends after a set time limit, or after a set number of turns.

16   Reaction Ball

Country: Luxembourg
Type: Ball
Players: 2
Age: 8–12
Equipment: 1 ball and
    2 traffic cones

FIGURE 4.18   At the word ''Hop!'' . . .

How to Play

Player "A" stands in the middle of his goal and faces away from the playing area. Player "B" starts about eight feet away with a ball and calls out, "Hop!" before he throws the ball toward the goal. At the word "Hop!" the goalie jumps around to face the shooter and in position to defend his goal. If Player "B" scores a goal he gets one point and steps back to the next line and has another turn. If Player "A" catches the ball before it goes into the goal, Player "B" must move back to the next line and attempt his second shot at the goal from there without receiving a point. This process is continued for five lines then players exchange positions. The player with the highest score wins the game.

17   Hoop Hunting

Country: Germany
Type: Ball
Players: 2
Age: 9–12
Equipment: 1 ball and
    1 hoop

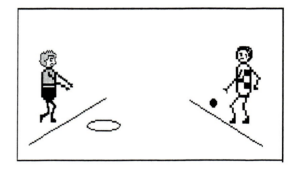

FIGURE 4.19   . . . and
tries to hit the hoop . . .

How to Play

Draw two lines about ten to twelve feet apart and place a hoop in the center. Player "A" throws the ball and tries to hit the hoop so that it will move toward Player "B" 's line. If Player "B" can catch the ball on the rebound he is allowed to throw the ball at the hoop. If he fails to catch the rebound, he must roll the ball across to Player "A" who then takes another turn. Game continues until the hoop has crossed a line. Player "B" begins the second game.

5

Games Involving Five Players

This new challenge expands the size of the group from two, as in the previous task, to five players. Because the challenge does not specify the type of pass to be used, each group has more freedom to determine whether they want to have a game that involves moving the ball with their feet or hands. The use of an unspecified small object also allows them to choose from a variety of small equipment, such as balls, beanbags, sticks, or stones. The last criteria in the challenge also specifies their new game will have to include a rule or movement that produces the required element of surprise. The following games fulfill the requirements of this challenge.

CHALLENGE: "SEE IF YOU CAN INVENT A GAME THAT HAS FIVE PLAYERS, PASSING A SMALL OBJECT, AND AN ELEMENT OF SURPRISE."

1   Quechibola

Country: Peru
Type: Ball
Players: 5
Age: 8–12
Equipment: 2 balls

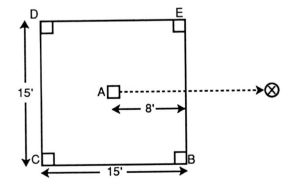

FIGURE 5.1   Quechibola

FIGURE 5.2 . . . player "A" runs with the ball . . .

How to Play

Arrange the playing area as shown in the diagram. Adjust distances according to the level of playing ability. Player "A" has one ball in his hand and one on the ground. He counts "one-two-three," then kicks the ball away from the four marked areas. As soon as the ball is kicked, player "E" runs after it while player "A" runs with the other ball to player "B." Player "B" takes the ball to player "C" while player "A" remains on player "B" 's spot. Players "C" and "D" continue the pattern until player "D" reaches player "A" 's spot and calls out, "Quechibola." If player "E" can fetch the ball and return to his spot and call "Quechibola" before player "D" reaches player "A," he exchanges positions with player "D." If player "D" reaches player "A" first, players "A–D" move one position counterclockwise and the game starts over.

2   Catch a Caterpillar

Country: England
Type: Manipulative
Players: 5
Age: 9–12
Equipment: 4 hoops, 1
   beanbag, and 1 stick

FIGURE 5.3   One player
stands in the middle . . .

How to Play

One player stands in the middle hoop and holds the stick in an upright position. The other four players stand inside their hoops. When ready, the outside players begin to pass the beanbag in a clockwise direction. When a player fails to catch the beanbag, the middle player holding the stick releases it. If the player who failed to catch the beanbag can grab the falling stick before it lands on the ground, he remains in his hoop. However, if he fails to catch the stick, he exchanges positions with the middle player.

3   Hidden Object

Country: Botswana
Type: Manipulative
Players: 5
Age: 8–10
Equipment: Small object

FIGURE 5.4   Hidden
Object

How to Play

One player hides his eyes while four players hide a small object, then tell the lone player to open his eyes. The four players then begin singing any song they know. While they are singing, the lone player begins to look for the object. If he moves closer to the hidden object, the others begin to sing louder; if he moves farther away, they sing softer. After the object is found, a new searcher is chosen and a new song must be selected by the group.

4   Beanbag Tag

Country: New Zealand
Type: Tag
Players: 5
Age: 7–12
Equipment: Beanbag

FIGURE 5.5   . . . and
places the beanbag in
one . . .

How to Play

Four players sit in a circle facing toward the center, eyes closed, and
hands behind their backs. "The fifth player" walks around the outside and
places the beanbag in one of the player's hands. "The fifth player" keeps
walking around the circle and when ready he calls, "Run to Safety!" All
players try to run to the designated safe area before the player with the
beanbag can tag another player. If a player is tagged he becomes the new
"fifth player."

5   Twelve Big Eggs

Country: Luxembourg
Type: Manipulative
Players: 5
Age: 9–12
Equipment: Medicine ball

FIGURE 5.6   Once the
player is standing on . . .

How to Play

Four players help the fifth onto a medicine ball. Once the player is standing on the ball, all other players run around her and try to get her to fall off the ball. They cannot push her, however, they can tickle or make funny faces. When the player falls off the ball, she must say, "Humpty Dumpty Stop!" to allow the other players time to run away. On "Stop," each player must turn around and stand with legs apart. "Humpty Dumpty" tries to roll the ball through any player's legs. If successful, she receives one point. Player number two takes her turn, and so on, until one player has accumulated twelve points ("twelve eggs").

6   Quick Number

Country: Japan
Type: Ball
Players: 5
Age: 8–12
Equipment: 1 beanbag

FIGURE 5.7   . . . rushes for the beanbag and calls . . .

How to Play

Players are numbered one to five and stand on a line five feet away from the wall. Player number one throws a beanbag against the wall and calls out a number. The player whose number is called rushes for the beanbag and calls, "Stop!" All players stop and the player tries to hit one of the other players below the waist with the beanbag. The player that is hit becomes "It" and all other players return to the starting line for the next turn.

7   Surprise, Surprise

Country: Wales
Type: Ball
Players: 5
Age: 7–9
Equipment: 1 ball

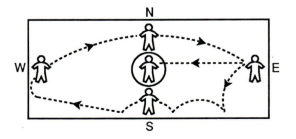

FIGURE 5.8   Surprise, Surprise

How to Play

Four players form a circle and the fifth player is designated to be "It" and stands in the middle. Circle players may throw or bounce the ball to any other circle player. If the middle player touches or catches the ball as it is being passed, he exchanges positions with the player who passed the ball.

8   Back Pass the Beanbag

Country: Australia
Type: Manipulative
Players: 5
Age: 9–12
Equipment: 1 beanbag

FIGURE 5.9   . . . passing the beanbag between . . .

How to Play

One person is "It" and stands about three yards away from the other four players. She faces the opposite direction and counts to twenty. The other players stand with their hands behind their backs passing the beanbag between each other until "It" calls out "twenty." On that cue, "It" tries to tag one of the players as they all run away keeping their hands behind their backs, concealing the truth about which one of them has the beanbag. "It" must try to catch the player who has possession of the beanbag. During the game players may secretly pass the beanbag to each other. Once the player with the beanbag is caught, she becomes "It." If a player is tagged and doesn't have the beanbag, then she can rejoin the game.

9   Paola Berni (Lost Island)

Country: Italy

Type: Manipulative

Players: 5

Age: 7–9

Equipment: 1 balloon and
   5 hoops

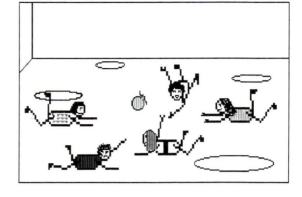

FIGURE 5.10   . . . move
on their stomachs . . .

How to Play

Arrange the class into groups of five and locate each group in a designated area of the gymnasium. Each player lies beside his hoop and one of these players has a balloon. On signal from the teacher, players begin to move on their stomachs and keep hitting the balloon into the air. When the teacher calls "Home," players stand up and run to their hoop (island). On the next turn, as the players are moving on their stomachs and hitting the balloon, the teacher removes one "island" from each group. This time when she calls "Home," players run to any "island." The player who cannot find an "island" is out of the game. The game continues until one player remains and is declared the winner.

10   Through the Obstacle

Country: Barbados

Type: Manipulative

Players: 5

Age: 7–12

Equipment: 1 ball, 1 chair,
   and a small object

FIGURE 5.11   Each player
tries to roll the ball . . .

How to Play

Five players line up behind a starting line. The distance is adjusted according to the level of ability of the children. At an appropriate distance away, a chair is placed facing the players with a small object (the target) sitting on the floor on the other side of the chair. Each player tries to roll the ball through the legs of the chair and hit the target. If a player hits the target, he gets one point and goes to the end of the line. The first player to receive five points wins the game.

11   One-Legged Concentration

Country: South Africa

Type: Ball

Players: 5

Age: 8–12

Equipment: 1 ball or beanbag and 4 traffic cones

FIGURE 5.12   The player with the beanbag . . .

How to Play

Arrange four traffic cones in a square and place one player in the middle and each of the other four players next to a traffic cone. The player in the center has a beanbag and calls out, "Go!" Every player, including the center player, starts hopping on one leg to a different traffic cone. The player with the beanbag can throw it to another player at any time. Players cannot stop hopping until they reach another traffic cone, so they have to catch the beanbag while moving. If a fair throw is made and a player catches it, she gets one point. If she drops or misses the beanbag she loses one point and must pick it up and throw it to another player. Two or more players cannot be at a cone at the same time. The game is restarted when all players are at a cone. The player who receives ten points first wins the game.

12 Katter (Cats)

Country: Sweden
Type: Manipulative
Players: 5
Age: 7–10
Equipment: 1 small object

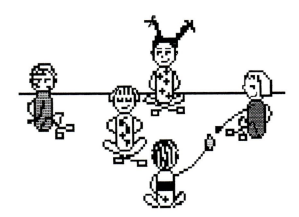

FIGURE 5.13 The center player closes his eyes . . .

How to Play

Four children sit cross-legged in a small circle. One player sits the same way in the center of the circle. The center player closes his eyes and counts out loud to ten while the circle players pass the beanbag behind their backs. The center player opens his eyes, remains in his sitting position, and tries to locate the child who has the beanbag. The circle players continue passing the beanbag, but if a player is caught with it, he exchanges places with the center player, and the game starts from the beginning.

13 Spell and Catch

Country: United States
Type: Ball
Players: 5
Age: 8–12
Equipment: 1 beanbag or
   ball

FIGURE 5.14 If he says the wrong letter . . .

How to Play

Five players form a circle with one player holding the ball. Before the game begins, each player must think of a word to be spelled. The game begins when player number one says his word, such as "Elephant," and calls out the first letter as he throws the ball to any circle player. The catching player must call out the second letter of the word before tossing the ball to another player. If he says the wrong letter he tosses the ball and must run twice around the circle before rejoining the game. The next player must say the correct second letter, and so on, before the third letter is called out. Any word chosen must be more than five letters. This provides for the final rule, that all players must participate in at least one letter of each word. Repeat game for each player's word.

14   Pass Ball

Country: Canada
Type: Ball
Players: 5
Age: 8–12
Equipment: 1 ball

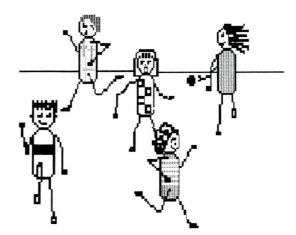

FIGURE 5.15   . . . player with the ball may try . . .

How to Play

Four players form a circle and the fifth player stands in the middle. One player in the circle has a ball and says, "Go!" Circle players begin to run counterclockwise and, at any time, the player with the ball may try to hit the middle player below the waist with it. The middle player may dodge, jump, or use any other movement to avoid being hit. When the middle player is hit, he exchanges positions with the player who hit him.

15   Foot Searching

Country: Belgium
Type: Manipulative
Players: 5
Age: 9–12
Equipment: 1 beanbag

FIGURE 5.16 . . . pass a
beanbag backwards with
their . . .

How to Play

Five players lie on their backs, one behind the other, in a straight line. The children pass a beanbag backwards with their feet. If a player drops the beanbag, it is returned to the front player and the game continues. When the beanbag arrives at the last child, this player runs to the beginning of the row, lies down, and the game starts again. The game is over when the first child arrives again at the beginning of the row.

16   Fir Cone Hide

Country: Luxembourg
Type: Manipulative
Players: 5
Age: 8–12
Equipment: 2 fir cones or
    small objects

FIGURE 5.17 At the
same time as the player
leaves . . .

How to Play

Four players stand in a circle and pass the two fir cones around the circle. The fifth player, called "The Warden," runs about twenty to thirty paces away from the other players, stops, and without looking back calls "Stop!" The circle player who is holding or about to receive the two fir cones, runs to "The Warden" and gives him one of the cones. At the same time as the player leaves the circle with the two cones, the other circle players run and hide behind any available cover. The two cone holders try to find the hidden players. The player who finds the most hidden players becomes the new "Warden."

17   Patty Wack

Country: Canada
Type: Manipulative
Players: 5
Age: 8–12
Equipment: 1 beanbag or
  ball

FIGURE 5.18   Patty Wack

FIGURE 5.19   ''Ready!''

How to Play

Four players assume a square formation with about eight feet between players and begin to pass a beanbag in a counterclockwise direction. The fifth player stands a few yards away and with his back to the group, and whenever he feels like it, gives the signal, "Patty Wack!" The person who has the beanbag stays in his position until all other players are lined up behind player number five. Number five calls, "Ready!" and the player with the beanbag must crawl through the tunnel and receive a few gentle patty wacks on his behind.

18   Merry-Go-Round

Country: Germany

Type: Manipulative

Players: 5

Age: 8–12

Equipment: 1 skipping rope
    and 1 beanbag

FIGURE 5.20   . . . other
players must jump over . . .

How to Play

The beanbag is tied to the end of the skipping rope. One player pulls the rope around him in a circular motion while the four other players must jump over it. The rope may be raised or lowered and moved faster or slower according to the wishes of the rope turner. If a person is touched by the rope he replaces the player in the center.

6

Games Involving the Whole Class

This challenge expands the number of participants in the game from five to the whole class. Making up a game for a large number of players is much more difficult than one involving five or six players or less. Therefore, to make this task easier, it is limited to a tag game that involves three small pieces of equipment. The games presented in the following pages demonstrate how children interpret the challenge in their own creative way and then devise very different and exciting tag activities.

CHALLENGE: "CAN YOU INVENT A NEW TAG GAME FOR YOUR CLASS? YOUR GAME MUST USE THREE STICKS" (substitute any other small equipment).

1   Hunter and Wolf

Country: Germany
Type: Run and tag
Players: Class
Age: 8–10
Equipment: 1 hoop, 3 sticks, and 3–4 small utility or nerf balls

FIGURE 6.1   If a "Wolf" is hit . . .

How to Play

Divide the class into two teams. The "Hunters" guard the camp and the "Wolves" try to knock down the camp fire (sticks). If a "Wolf" is hit by a ball, he must sit down and not interfere with the game. The game ends when the last "Wolf" is seated or the camp fire is knocked down. Change positions and start a new game.

2   Tag Bag

Country: England

Type: Tag

Players: Class

Age: 7–12

Equipment: 3 beanbags and
   3 hoops

FIGURE 6.2

FIGURE 6.3   "It" players
try to tag . . .

How to Play

One player takes three beanbags and throws them randomly inside the playing area. A hoop is placed around each beanbag. Three players are chosen to be "It" and pick up a beanbag. "It" players try to tag other players and, if successful, they give their beanbags to the new "It" and the game continues. During the game each player has five lives, which means he can go into the hoops (safe area) five times during the game.

3   Magic Ray Gun

Country: New Zealand
Type: Tag
Players: Class
Age: 9–12
Equipment: 3 sticks

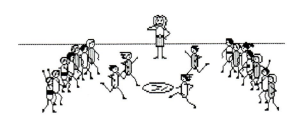

FIGURE 6.4   Since there
are only three . . .

How to Play

Divide the class into two equal teams and give each player on both teams
a number. The teams begin on opposite ends of the field. Place the sticks
in the circle located in the center of the field. The teacher calls out two
numbers and the four children with these numbers run to the middle to
retrieve the stick and become the "Killers." Since there are only three sticks,
one team has an advantage over the other on the basis of how many sticks
they picked up. As soon as the "Magic Ray Guns" are picked up, both teams
run as fast as they can to the other end of the field. If a player with a gun
tags an opponent, he must sit down where he was tagged. The team with
the most players reaching the end line is the winner.

4   Three Sticks

Country: Botswana
Type: Relay
Players: Class
Age: 8–10
Equipment: 3 sticks

FIGURE 6.5   . . . players
run around the . . .

How to Play

The class is divided into three equal teams and the first player of each
team holds a stick. On signal, "Go," players run around the markers which
are about twenty to thirty feet away and back to the next player. The first
team to finish wins the relay.

5   Three Pin Tag

Country: China
Type: Tag
Players: Class
Age: 9–12
Equipment: 3 traffic cones

FIGURE 6.6   . . . and must
run around the three . . .

How to Play

Arrange three traffic cones about three to four feet apart. One child is chosen to be "It" and the remaining players must stay within the designated playing area. When a player is tagged by "It," he becomes the new "It" and must run around the three traffic cones and back before he can try to tag another player. If the game is too slow, shorten the distance between each traffic cone, or add two more taggers.

6   Help

Country: Scotland
Type: Tag
Players: Class
Age: 7–12
Equipment: 3 sticks

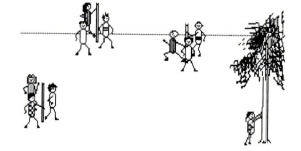

FIGURE 6.7   When
everyone is ready . . .

How to Play

One player is chosen to be the "Catcher." Three sticks are placed in the ground and numbered one, two, and three. The "Catcher" stands facing the tree or any suitable "home." All other players select one stick and stand beside it. When everyone is ready one of the players calls, "Help." The

"Catcher" calls a number, "one, two, or three," and the players at that stick must run to another stick without being tagged. Any player who is caught joins the "Catcher" and helps catch the remaining players the next time around. The last player to be tagged wins the game.

7   Stick Hunter

Country: Sweden
Type: Tag
Players: Class
Age: 7–12
Equipment: 3 sticks

FIGURE 6.8   . . . when a
player is about to . . .

How to Play

Three sticks are given to three children. One of the remaining players who does not have a stick is chosen to be the "Hunter." On signal from the teacher, the "Hunter" tries to tag another player. Any player who holds a stick cannot be tagged and, when a player is about to be tagged, he can be saved if one of the stick holders hands him a stick. However, only one person at a time is allowed to hold each stick. When a player is fairly tagged, he becomes the new "Hunter" and calls out, "I am the new Hunter," before he may chase another player.

8   Charge

Country: Australia
Type: Tag
Players: Class
Age: 9–12
Equipment: 3 sticks

FIGURE 6.9   . . . who may
charge at any time . . .

How to Play

Two players are chosen to be the "Guards" of the sticks (treasure) which are placed on the ground one yard inside the boundary line (to allow players to go behind them). The two guards try to prevent the sticks from being captured by the other players, who may charge at any time to get the sticks. Charging players, however, can only run and dodge while trying to grab the sticks; they cannot touch the "Guards." A "Guard" may leave his post to tag a player who has picked up a stick. If the "Guard" tags the player, that player is out of the game unless she has reached home fort on the other side of the playing area. When a player is caught the stick is returned to the original position for another "charge." The game is over when the "treasure" (three sticks) have been successfully stolen.

9   Scout Ball

Country: Italy
Type: Ball
Players: Class
Age: 10–12
Equipment: Class set of
    ribbons, 1 ball, and
    2 goals

FIGURE 6.10   When a
player has the ball . . .

How to Play

Divide the class into two teams. All players tuck a ribbon into the back of their shorts. Scout ball is played on an open field, with goals set at either end. A player can take five steps with the ball, then he must pass it to a teammate. The object is to carry the ball through the "goal posts." The opponents try to intercept the ball as it is being passed from player to player. When a player has the ball, he can be "scalped," that is, lose the colored ribbon tucked into his shorts. When this happens, the ball goes to the nearest opponent and the player leaves the field for one minute. After one minute he replaces his ribbon and rejoins the game. One point is awarded each time the attacking team can move the ball through their opponent's goal.

10   Surround Tag

Country: Japan
Type: Tag
Players: Class
Age 8–12
Equipment: 3 sticks

FIGURE 6.11   When a
player is surrounded . . .

How to Play

Three players are chosen to be the "Taggers" and each is given a stick. All other players must stay within the designated playing area. The three "Taggers" try to surround a player. When a player is surrounded by three players, he exchanges positions with one of the "Taggers." The method of selecting which one of the "Taggers" to exchange positions is decided by the following procedure. The tagged player thinks of a number between one and ten and the "Tagger" who guesses closest to the number, exchanges positions.

11   Headband Tag

Country: Argentina
Type: Tag
Players: Class
Age: 8–10
Equipment: Red and yellow
  bands

FIGURE 6.12   . . . players
begin to run anywhere . . .

How to Play

Two "Taggers" are selected and each given a headband to wear (yellow or red). The rest of the class are "Runners." In each of the four corners of the playing area are bags containing yellow and red headbands. On signal from the teacher, players begin to run anywhere in the designated playing area. When a player is tagged, he runs to the corner and picks up a headband which is the color of the player who tagged him. He then places the headband on and becomes another "Tagger." The game ends when everyone is wearing a headband, and the "Tagger" who gathered the most headbands is the winner.

12   Go for It

Country: United States
Type: Tag
Players: Class
Age: 8–12
Equipment: 3 sticks

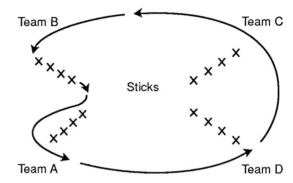

FIGURE 6.13   Go for It

FIGURE 6.14   . . . players all run in the same . . .

How to Play

The class is divided into four equal teams. All players of each team sit down except the first player in each line. On signal from the teacher, the first players race to pick up a stick from the center of the playing area. After picking up the stick, the players all run in the same direction around the outside of the four teams (counterclockwise), replace the stick in the center, return to the back of their team's line, and sit down. When they complete this they receive one point for their team. A player who does not pick up a stick must run in the same direction and try to tag a player who has a stick. If he tags one of these players, the tagged player must give him his stick and walk to the back of his own team. Play continues until everyone has had a turn and the team with the highest number of points wins the game.

13   Stick and Chain Tag

Country: Belgium
Type: Tag
Players: Class
Age: 8–12
Equipment: 3 sticks

FIGURE 6.15   . . . he must hold on to the free . . .

How to Play

Three players are selected to be "Taggers" and each is given a stick. All other players must stay within the designated playing area. When the teacher says, "Go," the "Taggers" try to tag as many players with their sticks as possible. When each player is tagged, he must hold on to the free hand of the "Tagger" or the hand of the last player in the chain of players behind the "Tagger." The last person caught wins the game.

14   Stick Tag

Country: Canada
Type: Tag
Players: Class
Age: 7–10
Equipment: 3 sticks about 6 to 8 feet long and 3 to 5 ribbons

FIGURE 6.16   A player is safe when . . .

How to Play

Three sticks are randomly placed in the designated playing area and three to five players are chosen to be "Taggers." "Taggers" wear ribbons and begin to chase other players. A player is safe when she is balancing on one foot on the stick. Any number of players may balance on the stick and remain as long as they like, providing they maintain the one foot balance position.

15   Wizard

Country: Peru
Type: Tag
Players: Class
Age: 8–12
Equipment: 3 sticks

FIGURE 6.17   As soon as a player . . .

How to Play

One player is chosen to be the "Wizard" and stands in the middle of the playing area with three sticks. All other players must scatter in the playing area. The "Wizard" calls out "one-two-three," then begins to chase after the players. As soon as a player is touched with a stick, she must take it and become another "Wizard." The game continues for a few minutes, then a new "Wizard" is chosen and given the three sticks to begin the game.

16   Cold Winds

Country: England
Type: Tag
Players: Class
Age: 7–10
Equipment: 3 colored
   ribbons

FIGURE 6.18   . . . and hold his hands . . .

How to Play

Three players are chosen to be the "Taggers" and stand in the middle of the playing area. They tuck a colored ribbon in their shorts. All other players scatter in the playing area. On signal from the teacher, the "Taggers" try to tag as many players as possible. When a player is tagged, he must stand still and hold his hands above his head. Tagged players can be rescued if another player can circle him before being tagged. The game continues until all players are standing with their hands above their heads.

17   Hot Stick Tag

Country: South Africa
Type: Tag
Players: Class
Age: 9–12
Equipment: 3 small sticks

FIGURE 6.19   "It" tries to tag any player . . .

How to Play

Three players are given a stick and one of the remaining players in the class is chosen to be "It." All players scatter anywhere in the playing area. On signal from the teacher, "It" tries to tag any player who has a stick. However, to avoid being tagged, a player who has a stick may pass it to any player at any time. Players must accept the stick or they automatically become "It." When a player is tagged, she must call out "I am It!" and the game continues.

7

Games from a Teacher's Special Challenge

The challenges presented in the previous three chapters were designed to gradually introduce children to a new method of creating their own games. The first challenge involved two players and limited options concerning rules and skills. The challenges in Chapters 5 and 6 increased the size of the group the game was created for and allowed greater variety in the selection of small equipment.

The fourth challenge given to the children was an open one to allow each teacher to design an individual challenge. This opportunity permitted each teacher to adjust the task to the age and cultural background of the class. It also allowed teachers to use any special facilities or equipment that were available locally. Finally, and perhaps most important, it gave each teacher an opportunity to make a personal creative contribution to this project. The games that follow indicate how well teachers adapted to new methods of teaching and how they used these methods to stimulate the creative talents of their students.

CHALLENGE: NOTE TO TEACHER: MAKE UP YOUR OWN CHALLENGE. YOU MAY DECIDE ON THE NUMBER OF PLAYERS, AS WELL AS IMPOSE LIMITATIONS RELATING TO SPACE, EQUIPMENT, SKILLS, AND RULES.

1   Gold

Country: England
Type: Ball
Players: 10–20
Age: 7–12
Equipment: Beanbag

FIGURE 7.1   . . . before
he throws the beanbag . . .

Teacher's Challenge: "Can you invent a game which has chasing in it?
You must use a beanbag in your game, and at
some time, you must throw it."

How to Play

One player is given the beanbag (gold) and begins to run anywhere
within the playing area. All other players begin to chase after and try to tag
him before he throws the beanbag in any direction. If he is tagged while
holding the beanbag, he is "killed" and must remain standing with legs
apart until the end of the game. The player who tags him takes the gold,
runs off in another direction, and repeats the action. If a player throws the
gold before being tagged and no other player is willing to pick it up, the
player who threw it picks it up and throws it again. The game continues
until two players remain and are declared the winners.

2 Four Squares

Country: Barbados
Type: Ball
Players: Class
Age: 10–12
Equipment: 1 large ball

FIGURE 7.2 The game is started with a jump ball . . .

Teacher's Challenge: "Can you design a basketball game for the whole class that uses one large ball? Players may walk but cannot run with the ball. All other basketball rules apply."

How to Play

The class is divided into four teams with two players from each team assigned to guard their own home square (six feet by six feet). The diagonally opposite home square is each team's opponent's home square. Players from any team may scatter anywhere they wish in the playing area. The game is started with a jump ball between four opposing players. A point is scored every time a ball touches an opponent's home square.

3 Pair Tag

Country: Greece
Type: Tag
Players: Class
Age: 7–12
Equipment: None

Tigers!

FIGURE 7.3 When the "Hunter" calls the . . .

Teacher's Challenge: "See if you can make up a tag game that requires all players, except the 'Tagger' to be in partners."

How to Play

One player is chosen to be the "Hunter." All other players form pairs, hold hands, and stand in their own circle marked on the ground. Each pair calls out or is given the name of an animal. When the "Hunter" calls the name of one or more animals, pairs with those names must keep holding hands, run around three other circles, and back to their own circle. If the "Hunter" tags a pair before they return to their circle, they are out of the game. The last pair remaining in the game is declared the winner.

4   Piggy Back Polo

Country: Botswana
Type: Manipulative and ball
Players: Class
Age: 9–12
Equipment: 1 ball

FIGURE 7.4   Players on the outside circle . . .

Teacher's Challenge: "Try and discover a game that the whole class can play and must use a throw and a catch."

How to Play

The class is divided into partners of equal size and weight. Partners then form a double circle with one child in the middle holding a ball. Players on the outside circle jump onto their partner's back. When everyone is ready, the player in the center throws the ball to any mounted player. These players continue to throw to any other mounted player. When a player makes a poor throw or drops the ball, he changes position with the player in the middle. Before the new middle player throws the ball, all pairs reverse positions.

5   Nirali Batel (King)

Country: India
Type: Ball and tag
Players: Class
Age: 9–12
Equipment: 1 ball

FIGURE 7.5   Nirali Batel

Teacher's Challenge: "Design a game for the whole class using one ball
                     and a throw."

How to Play

One player is chosen to start the game. He throws the ball and tries to
hit another player. Players must remain inside the square (forty feet by forty
feet) and use their fists to prevent their bodies from being hit. They also
use their fists to hit the ball toward another player. Any player hit must move
outside the square. If the ball goes out of the square, the last person to hit
it, or any player who is out of the game, may retrieve it and throw it back
into the square. Game continues until one player, the "King," remains.

6   One-Two-Three Tag

Country: Japan
Type: Tag
Players: Class
Age: 8–12
Equipment: None

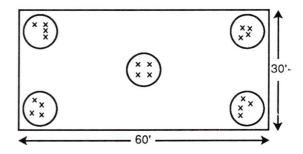

FIGURE 7.6   One-Two-
Three Tag

Teacher's Challenge: "See if you can invent a new tag game where no
                     player is eliminated."

How to Play

Four circles are drawn near the four corners of the playing area and one in the middle. Place four taggers in the center circle and equal numbers of players in the outer circles, using the whole class. One tagger in the center circle is designated to give a whistle command that all four groups must follow. These are:

one whistle: all groups move to the next circle on their right.

two whistles: all groups move to the next circle on their left.

three whistles: all groups remain in their own circles.

On the first two commands, taggers try to tag the players before they reach the next circle. If a player moves out of his present circle on three whistles, he moves to the center circle and becomes a tagger. After five or six signals, the outer circle with the most players wins the game.

7   Kangaroo

Country: Peru
Type: Manipulative
Players: 2–4
Age: 8–12
Equipment: 1 beanbag

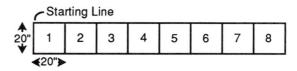

FIGURE 7.7   Kangaroo

FIGURE 7.8   She hops on one foot . . .

FIGURE 7.9   . . . using the
same foot . . .

FIGURE 7.10   . . . holding
the beanbag between . . .

Teacher's Challenge: "Let's see if you can organize a game where each
player will do the same thing. First, each of you
must jump continuously on one foot and later on
both feet. Also, you are to use a small object."

How to Play

The playing area is marked as shown in the diagram; each player takes
a turn one after the other. The first player begins by facing the marked area
and throwing a beanbag into area one. She then hops on one foot into each
area and back to area one, picks up the beanbag, and hops out. This procedure is repeated for areas one to eight and back. If she does not throw
the beanbag into the correct area, changes her hopping action, or fails to
pick up the beanbag, she loses her turn. After all players have had their
turn, each person starts again in the area where he/she made an error.

The second phase of this game begins with the players throwing the beanbag into area one. Next, he hops into this area and, using the same foot he is standing on, pushes the beanbag into area two and so on to area eight and back to the starting position. If the beanbag goes out-of-bounds or if it does not stop inside each area, the player loses his turn. On his next turn, each player returns to the area where he made an error.

The third phase begins with the player holding the beanbag between her knees. Keeping the beanbag in this position, she jumps into each area one after the other and then back to the starting position. She cannot touch the beanbag with any other part of her body during this phase. If she drops the beanbag, lands on a line, or misses an area, she loses her turn. Like the previous two phases, on her next turn she returns to the area where she made an error.

8   Bumper Boats

Country: South Africa
Type: Manipulative
Players: Class
Age: 8–10
Equipment: None

FIGURE 7.11   . . . they must run around the boundaries . . .

Teacher's Challenge: "Invent a game where two players are joined together. No equipment is to be used and no one is to be eliminated from the game."

How to Play

The class is arranged in partners who are seated, facing each other and holding onto each other's ankles. Partners then move around the playing area in this position and try to force other pairs to lose their balance and fall sideways or to release their grip on their partners ankles. If any pair commits any of these fouls, they must run around the boundaries of the playing area before rejoining the game.

9   One-Two-Three Catch Me

Country: Luxembourg
Type: Tag
Players: 5–6 on each team
Age: 9–12
Equipment: None

FIGURE 7.12   . . . with
their hands stretched
out . . .

Teacher's Challenge: "Can you make up a new tag game for ten to twelve
players?"

How to Play

   Arrange two teams, of five to six players each, on opposite lines drawn
about ten yards apart. Player number one from Team A runs across to the
other team who are standing behind their line with their hands stretched
out to be tagged. Player number one must tap three hands then turn and
run back across her own line. After the third tap, the whole opposing team
runs after player number one. If she is tagged before reaching her own line,
she becomes a prisoner and must stand behind the opposing team. If she
makes it across her own line before being tagged, the last person tapped
becomes her prisoner. Teams alternate turns and continue to the last player
on each team. The team with the most prisoners wins the game.

10   Beats Me

Country: England
Type: Manipulative
Players: 10
Age: 8–12
Equipment: 1 mat, 1 ball,
   and 1 hoop

FIGURE 7.13   . . . throws
the ball to the first . . .

FIGURE 7.14 Beats Me

Teacher's Challenge: "Is it possible to invent a game that has five players on each team, a mat, a ball, and a hoop?"

How to Play

Each team has five players and are designated as the "Batting" and the "Fielding" teams. Each member of the "Batting" team is allowed one fair pitch before teams exchange positions. The pitcher or bowler of the "Fielding" team throws the ball to the first batter. If the batter hits the ball, she performs a forward roll over the mat, runs around the hoop, and performs another forward roll. She must do these movements before the "Fielding" team can retrieve the ball and return it to the pitcher who must remain inside the hoop. Teams exchange positions after the third batter has had her turn.

11 Ball in Boxes

Country: Jamaica
Type: Ball
Players: 8
Age: 7–10
Equipment: 4 balls and
   4 boxes

FIGURE 7.15   . . . throw
the ball into the box . . .

Teacher's Challenge: "Make up a game that has eight players, four balls, and four boxes."

How to Play

The group is divided into four teams and each team has a "Thrower" and a "Catcher." On signal from the teacher, the "Thrower" tries to throw the ball into the box held by the "Catcher." The "Catcher" can help the "Thrower" by lowering and raising the box to catch the ball. As soon as the ball is caught, partners change positions and the game continues. The first team to score ten points wins the game.

12   Avoid the Circle

Country: Wales
Type: Tag
Players: 6–8
Age: 9–12
Equipment: 1 ball

FIGURE 7.16   Avoid the Circle

Teacher's Challenge: "Make up a game with ten players and using one ball."

How to Play

One player is selected to be "A" and stands in the middle of the circle. All circle players are named "B1" to the last number. On signal "Go," "A" tries to tag any circle player. Once a circle player is caught, she becomes known as "C" player and must go to the center of the circle. If "C" can bounce a ball five times in a row, she becomes a "B" player again. If she fails to bounce the ball the correct number of times, she becomes player "A." The game starts over after a child successfully bounces the ball five times. If a player is caught a second time, she must hop on one foot while bouncing the ball. When caught the third time, she hops on one foot with eyes closed while bouncing the ball. Make up your own rules for a player caught the fourth or fifth time.

13   Bokstarsboll (Letter Ball)

Country: Sweden
Type: Manipulative
Players: 4–5
Age: 7–9
Equipment: 2 hoops and
     1 ball

FIGURE 7.17   The first
player in the line . . .

Teacher's Challenge: "See if you can make up a game with two hoops,
               five players, one ball, and one element of
               guesswork."

How to Play

   One child holds a hoop in front of himself and directly over another
hoop on the ground. The other players line up behind a line drawn six to
ten feet away from the hoop. The child holding the hoop thinks of the
name of an animal. He may, depending on the maturity of the players, give
some hints such as "It's small and white . . . and it flies." The first player
in the line tries to throw the ball into the upper hoop so it will land in the
hoop on the floor. If it lands inside the second hoop, he tries to guess the
first letter of the animal's name. If correct, he gets another try for the second
letter and so on. If he answers incorrectly, the next player takes his turn.
The game continues until a player spells the full name of the animal.

14   War

Country: New Zealand
Type: Ball
Players: Class
Age: 9–12
Equipment: 15 utility balls

FIGURE 7.18   On signal
from the teacher . . .

Teacher's Challenge: "Can you design a game for the whole class using
               fifteen utility balls?"

How to Play

Divide the class into two teams and assign each a home area. Place fifteen utility balls on the center line. On signal from the teacher, any number of players from each team may rush forward and pick up one or more balls. The object of the game is to hit the opponent below the waist with a ball. A player can be hit while in any part of the playing area. However, attacking players cannot advance beyond the opponent's home base line. When a player is fairly hit, he must stand on the side or end line and may pass the ball to his teammates but may not throw the ball at an opponent. Any player may retrieve a ball that has gone out-of-bounds, but must always throw it to a teammate.

15   Stolen Ball

Country: Argentina
Type: Ball and tag
Players: Class
Age: 10–12
Equipment: 1 ball

FIGURE 7.19   If a player reaches her opponent's . . .

Teacher's Challenge: "Imagine a game in which all the class participates
                      and which takes place on a football field with
                      one ball."

How to Play

Divide the class into two equal teams and arrange each team as shown in the illustration. One ball is placed in each goal. A safety zone is marked three yards in front of each goal and parallel to the center line. The aim of the game is for each team to steal their opponent's ball and bring it back to their own safety zone. Players on each team cannot be tagged in their own half of the field. When a player crosses the center line and is tagged before she reaches her opponent's safety zone, she must remain in place until another "untouched" teammate tags her free. If a player reaches her opponent's safety zone she cannot be tagged while remaining in this area. This player, and any other teammate who is in their opponent's safety zone, may pick up the ball and try to run back across to their own half of the field without being tagged. These players may pass the ball back and forth as they run through their opponent's half of the field. However, if they are tagged or drop the ball, they must stay where they were tagged and the ball is returned to their opponent's goal. One point is scored for each successful stolen ball. The game starts over after each point is scored.

16   Empire Strikes Back

Country: Canada
Type: Manipulative
Players: Class
Age: 8–12
Equipment: Class set of
   hoops and utility balls

FIGURE 7.20   . . . which
he kicks trying to hit . . .

Teacher's Challenge: "Make up a game for the class that has one hoop
                  and a utility ball for each player."

How to Play

The players are scattered throughout the playing area. Everyone except
"It" has a hoop which they hold around their waist and use as a spaceship.
These people are the "Forces of Evil" and "It" belongs to the "Good Side."
"It" has a utility ball which he kicks trying to hit the "Forces of Evil" flying
about in their spaceships. "Forces of Evil" who are hit with a ball then trade
in their hoop for a ball and become a member of the "Good Side." The
game ends when all the "Forces of Evil" are caught.

17   Check Mate

Country: United States
Type: Manipulative
Players: 7–9
Age: 7–9
Equipment: 4 blindfolds and
   4 small objects

FIGURE 7.21   They use this
method to guide . . .

Teacher's Challenge: "Invent a game for the class where one or more
                  members are blindfolded."

How to Play

Divide the class into four teams and place four objects in the middle of the playing area. Blindfold one member of each team and have team members turn this person around three times. Each group decides on a method of communicating by sound that does not use words (such as clapping, hissing, or whistling). They then use this method to guide their blindfolded teammate to the center, to pick up an object, and to bring it back to the group. The first person back wins the game for his team.

18   Columbola

Country: Peru
Type: Ball
Players: 6
Age: 7–10
Equipment: 1 ball and 1 goal

FIGURE 7.22   . . . and the
first person on each . . .

Teacher's Challenge: "Organize a game with six players, throwing the
                       ball, and one goal."

How to Play

Two teams line up on each side of the bench, facing the field of play. The teacher throws the ball as far as possible and the first person on each team runs after it. The first person to pick it up gets a free throw at the goal while his opponent must stand still. If the ball goes through the goal, his team gets one point and the next players in line take their turn. If the ball does not go through the goal, both players run after it and continue the game until someone scores a goal.

19   Spacehopper Flight

Country: Germany
Type: Manipulative
Players: 2
Age: 8–10
Equipment: 2 spacehoppers
  and 2 darts or pieces of
  chalk

FIGURE 7.23   . . . prevent
the other players from . . .

Teacher's Challenge: "See if you can make up a game with your friend
and use the spacehoppers."

How to Play

Each player sits on her spacehopper and holds a suction dart or piece
of chalk. The object of this game is to attach the dart (or make a mark with
the chalk) on the opponent's spacehopper and to prevent the other player
from attaching a dart to your spacehopper. One point for each successful
touch and the first player to score five points wins the game.

20   Chase Me

Country: China
Type: Tag
Players: Class
Age: 8–12
Equipment: None

FIGURE 7.24   . . . the
"Runner" tries to run and
stand . . .

Teacher's Challenge: "Can you make up a tag game for the whole class
involving partners in some way?"

How to Play

The class is arranged into partners standing one behind the other and scattered throughout the playing area. One player is selected to be "It." Another player is chosen to be the "Runner" who stands behind any set of partners. On signal, the "Runner" tries to run and stand in front of another group while the "It" tries to tag her. If the "Runner" is tagged before she reaches her target, she exchanges places with "It" and the game continues in the same manner. If the "Runner" successfully reaches her target, the player at the rear of this set of partners becomes the new "Runner" and must start to run to the front of a new set with "It" now trying to tag her.

21   Change the Spot

Country: Australia
Type: Tag
Players: Class
Age: 8–12
Equipment: None

FIGURE 7.25   . . . change
to a hop . . .

Teacher's Challenge: "Can you make up a game for the whole class but without using any equipment?"

How to Play

Mark off a playing area about twenty yards square. One player is chosen to be "It" and all other players scatter in the playing area. "It" picks three danger marks on the floor and tells the teacher where they are located. The remainder of the class does not know where these danger spots are. The game begins with a signal from "It," such as, "Run forward." As the players are moving, "It" may direct them to change directions or to change to a hop, run, or slide, etc. When a person steps on or crosses over the first danger spot, "It" calls that person's name, and that player must stop, call out his own name, then continue moving. "It" may continue to use the first danger spot or if she notices the class avoiding the spot, she will call out "Number two spot!" and continue changing locomotor movements and directions. The game continues until "It" has used her three danger spots and cannot catch any players.

22   Twirlies

Country: Scotland
Type: Manipulative - tag
Players: Class
Age: 7–9
Equipment: None

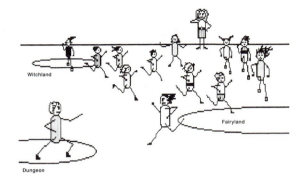

FIGURE 7.26   . . . if the
"Fairy Queen" can run . . .

Teacher's Challenge: "See if you can invent a tag game without any
equipment. If a player is tagged he can be
rescued in some way."

How to Play

Witchland, Fairyland, and the Dungeon are marked on the ground as
shown in the illustration. One player is chosen to be the "Witch" (tagger)
and another to be the "Fairy Queen." The other players start twirling around
near the center of the playing area with their eyes closed. As they twirl in
place, the teacher calls "Home," signaling the players to keep their eyes
closed but to stop twirling and begin to walk forward. As soon as a player
walks toward Witchland, the "Witch" must call out, "Open your eyes," signaling all players to open their eyes and run for Fairyland. If a player is
tagged before reaching Fairyland, she goes to the Dungeon. If the "Fairy
Queen" can run to the Dungeon and touch a tagged player before the
"Witch" tags her, both players have safe passage back to Fairyland. However, if the "Fairy Queen" is tagged by the "Witch" before she can touch
a tagged player, they exchange positions and the game starts over.

23   Pole Handball

Country: Canada
Type: Ball
Players: Class
Age: 10–12
Equipment: 1 ball,
   backboard, and 2 cones

FIGURE 7.27   The game
begins with . . .

Teacher's Challenge: "Can you make up a basketball game that does not
                    use the basket as a goal?"

How to Play

Divide class into two equal teams, however, if there are more than twelve
players per side, half of each team are designated as court players and the
other half as sideline players. The game begins with a jump ball at center.
Players may advance the ball only by throwing it; dribbling with hands or
kicking the ball is not allowed. Players must also pass the ball within three
seconds of receiving it. A goal is scored if the ball hits any part of the basketball backboard superstructure. The goalie may attempt to prevent the
ball from hitting the superstructure. If playing inside, the ball is live if it
hits the wall. Any foul, such as unnecessary roughness, travelling, or time
violations, is penalized by a penalty shot from the center of the court. The
penalty shot must be taken by a player who has not scored, and the goalie
may not defend the goal during a penalty shot. A sideline player may not
score but may receive and pass the ball to a sideline or court player. Sideline players rotate with court players every two minutes.

Part Three

New Cooperative Games

One dominant characteristic of the games children invented in Part Two was the competitive nature of their games. They would inevitably come up with a game that had a winner and a loser. Although this applied to virtually every country and every age group, the creation of such games is not due to a competitive instinct all children possess, but rather the result of the competitive model provided for them by adults from all countries.

In order to help children create games which were noncompetitive, a new column was added to the original Creative Games Chart. This column included four elements of cooperative behavior: participation, equality, success, and trust. Each teacher was instructed to teach the meaning of these elements before presenting the four creative game challenges. The cooperative games which resulted from these new challenges are described and illustrated in the next four chapters. These games clearly demonstrate that children, regardless of age or cultural background, can invent cooperative games that are exciting, safe, and enjoyable to play.

8

Games Involving Two Players and Stressing Equality and Trust

The following challenge, as well as those presented in the next three chapters, are not posed to children until they have answered the challenges presented in Part Two. This procedure is followed to help children gain experience in creating their own games before adding new cooperative dimensions. It also helps each teacher gain valuable experience in posing challenges involving different numbers of players, playing space, skills, and rules.

The first sentence in the following challenge allows the two players maximum freedom to select the number and type of equipment they want to use in their game. The two cooperative elements of equality and trust, specified in the second sentence, ensure that these two elements will be present in their game. In fact, the games presented in this chapter demonstrate that children invariably include at least three of the four elements of equality, trust, participation, and success.

CHALLENGE: "CAN YOU DESIGN A COOPERATIVE GAME WITH YOUR PARTNER USING ANY AVAILABLE EQUIPMENT? YOUR GAME MUST STRESS EACH PLAYER HAS AN *EQUAL* ROLE IN THE GAME AND MUST, IN SOME WAY, PLACE *TRUST* IN THE OTHER PLAYER."

1 Under Ball

Country: Botswana
Type: Ball
Players: 2
Age: 8–10
Equipment: 1 ball

FIGURE 8.1 . . . tries
to bounce the ball
between . . .

Cooperative Elements: [x] Equality   [x] Trust
                       [x] Participation [ ] Success

How to Play

One player stands with her legs apart while the other stands behind her
with a ball. The player with the ball tries to bounce it between her partner's
legs so she can catch it as it bounces up through her legs. The game continues with each player taking a turn bouncing and then catching the ball.

2 Jump Hoop

Country: England
Type: Manipulative
Players: 2
Age: 7–10
Equipment: 1 rope and
  3 hoops

FIGURE 8.2 . . . as player
"B" drags it across . . .

Cooperative Elements: [x] Equality   [x] Trust
                       [x] Participation [x] Success

How to Play

Place two hoops on the playing field about twenty feet apart. Player "A" stands in one hoop and player "B" drags a second hoop that is attached to a short rope alongside of player "A." The aim of the game is for player "A" to jump into player "B" 's hoop and remain inside this hoop as player "B" drags it across to the third hoop. This is accomplished by player "A" taking short steps or jumps as player "B" pulls the hoop toward the third hoop. Players change positions and repeat action back to the first hoop.

3   Fingertips

Country: Germany

Type: Manipulative

Players: 2

Age: 8–12

Equipment: Any available
   small equipment

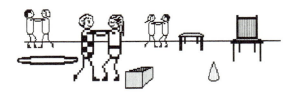

FIGURE 8.3   . . . they
guide each other
around . . .

Cooperative Elements: [x] Equality   [x] Trust
                        [x] Participation   [x] Success

How to Play

A series of obstacles such as boxes, hoops, and benches are scattered around the playing area. The class is organized into partners who stand randomly throughout the playing area, facing each other. Partner's lift their hands to shoulder level and lightly touch each other's shoulders. Now, without talking or using any other cues except through their fingertips, they guide each other around the obstacles by applying a little pressure through their fingers to let each other know whether they want to move forward, backward, right, left, up, or down. Game can continue in this fashion or with one partner keeping his eyes closed as they move throughout the obstacles.

4   Stick Exchange

Country: Japan
Type: Manipulative
Players: 2
Age: 8–12
Equipment: 2 sticks, each
approximately 3 feet in
length

FIGURE 8.4   Without using
their hands . . .

Cooperative Elements: [x] Equality   [x] Trust
                                     [x] Participation   [ ] Success

How to Play

Two players assume a crawling position and face each other. One player places a stick on his right shoulder while the other places the other end on his left shoulder. Without using their hands, they try to help each other move the stick to their other shoulder while gradually shifting to a standing position. After reaching a standing position, they try to reverse directions and return the stick to its original position. If either player uses his hands or if the stick drops off either player's shoulder, they must start from the beginning.

5   Double Tug

Country: South Africa
Type: Manipulative
Players: 2
Age: 8–12
Equipment: 2 beanbags and
1 hoop

FIGURE 8.5   . . . facing
each other and holding . . .

Cooperative Elements: [x] Equality   [x] Trust
                        [x] Participation   [ ] Success

How to Play

Two beanbags are placed in the middle of the hoop. Players pair off and stand inside the hoop facing each other and holding hands. They bend down and using their partner's handhold for mutual support, lean backwards, and hold this position. When in this position they reach forward and pick up a beanbag with their free hand, then return the beanbag to the middle of their hoop. The action is repeated with the players adding placing the beanbag on their head or any other part of their body.

6   Balance Challenge

Country: New Zealand

Type: Manipulative

Players: 2

Age: 9–12

Equipment: 2 traffic cones
   (skittles), 1 plank, and
   1 block of wood

FIGURE 8.6   . . . as they
walk to opposite ends . . .

Cooperative Elements: [x] Equality   [x] Trust
                        [x] Participation   [ ] Success

How to Play

Arrange equipment as shown in the illustration. Two players begin at the center of plank and must keep the plank off the floor as they walk to opposite ends, pick up the skittle, and return to the starting position. If they are successful, the next challenge is to repeat the activity while each partner is balancing a beanbag on their heads or throwing a ball back and forth as they move to the end and back.

7   Ball Thrower

Country: France

Type: Ball

Players: 2

Age: 9–12

Equipment: 1 bat, 1 tennis or
   sponge ball, and 6 skittles
   or bowling pins

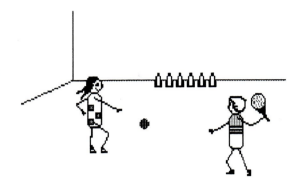

FIGURE 8.7   . . . bounces
the ball toward player "B."

Cooperative Elements: [x] Equality   [x] Trust
                        [x] Participation   [ ] Success

How to Play

   The equipment is arranged as shown in the illustration. Player "A"
bounces the ball toward player "B." Player "B" tries to bat the ball and
knock over as many skittles as possible. Players change position after each
throw. The challenge in this game is to try, as a pair, to knock all the skittles
over with the fewest number of throws.

8   Polo

Country: Argentina

Type: Manipulative

Players: 2

Age: 9–12

Equipment: 1 ball, 6 traffic
   cones, and 1 long stick

FIGURE 8.8   The "Horse"
carries the "Rider" . . .

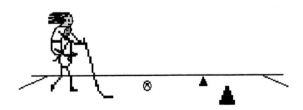

Cooperative Elements: [x] Equality   [x] Trust
                        [x] Participation   [ ] Success

How to Play

One player is designated as the "Horse" and the other as the "Rider." The "Horse" carries the "Rider" from the starting line to the end line. The "Rider" has a long stick in his hand which he uses to push the ball between the traffic cones. If he knocks a traffic cone over either by his stick or the ball, he must reset it. This is accomplished by joint effort; the "Rider" stays on the "Horse" and the "Horse" bends down so the "Rider" can reach the traffic cone and reset it while still mounted. Players exchange positions at the end line and repeat the activity back to the starting line.

9   Leap Ball

Country: Australia

Type: Ball

Players: 2

Age: 10–12

Equipment: 1 ball and
    1 hoop

FIGURE 8.9   Player one
begins in a leapfrog . . .

Cooperative Elements: [x] Equality   [x] Trust
                        [x] Participation   [ ] Success

How to Play

Two hoops are placed on the ground about thirty feet apart. Player one begins in a leapfrog position and player two rolls the ball through her legs, then leapfrogs over her. Player one repeats this action and so on, until they reach the opposite hoop. After reaching the hoop, one player begins to bounce the ball and, when the ball rebounds, the other partner makes the second bounce. Players keep alternating the bouncing movement until they return to the first hoop.

10   Hoopscotch

Country: Canada
Type: Manipulative
Players: 2
Age: 8–12
Equipment: 9 hoops or
    circles drawn in dirt area

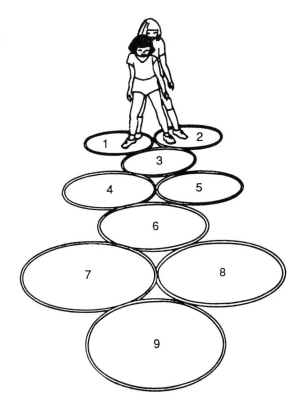

FIGURE 8.10

Cooperative Elements: [x] Equality   [x] Trust
                         [x] Participation   [x] Success

How to Play

The two players first arrange their hoops as shown in the drawing. Players then begin one behind the other, starting out with hands on the waist of the one in front, and facing hoops one and two. They jump together both landing with one foot in each hoop. Players jump again placing both feet in hoop three. Next, they jump and place one foot each in hoops four and five, and both their hands in hoop six. The next jump results with one foot each in hoops seven and eight. The last jump is into hoop nine, where both players land with both feet in the hoop. Players turn around and repeat the same movements back to the starting position.

11   Blind Horse

Country: Germany
Type: Manipulative
Players: 2
Age: 10–12
Equipment: 1 skipping rope,
   small equipment

FIGURE 8.11   . . . and
directs the "Horse"
through . . .

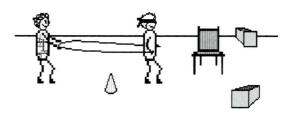

Cooperative Elements: [x] Equality   [x] Trust
                        [x] Participation   [ ] Success

How to Play

One child is blindfolded and holds the ends of the skipping rope at his
sides. The other player is the "Driver" and directs the "Horse" through a
series of obstacles scattered around the playing area by gently pulling on
the rope. Exchange positions every thirty seconds or whatever time schedule
agreed upon by the two players.

12   Blind Ball

Country: Belgium
Type: Ball
Players: 2
Age: 9–12
Equipment: 1 ball

FIGURE 8.12   . . . stops
then gives a verbal clue . . .

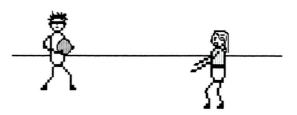

Cooperative Elements: [x] Equality   [x] Trust
                        [x] Participation   [ ] Success

How to Play

Two players stand about ten to twelve feet apart. Player "A" is blindfolded and holds the ball. Player "B" moves in any direction he wishes,
stops, then gives a verbal clue to where he is located. Player "A" throws
the ball to player "B," and he tries to catch it without moving his feet. Players
exchange positions after each throw and, if successful, extend the distance
on each sucessive throw, and change the clue to a clap or short whistle.

13   Two Noses

Country: Luxembourg

Type: Manipulative

Players: 2

Age: 7–12

Equipment: 1 small box or
small ball and 1 long
skipping rope

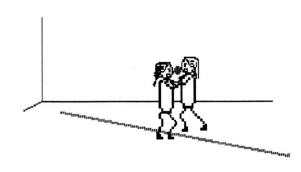

FIGURE 8.13   . . . across
the rope and between
their . . .

Cooperative Elements: [x] Equality   [x] Trust
                        [x] Participation [ ] Success

How to Play

A long rope is placed in a straight line on the floor. Two players stand on either side of the rope and hold a small object, such as a matchbox or nerf ball, across the rope and between their noses. The aim of the players is to stay on their own side of the rope and follow its path without dropping the object. If successful, the next attempts should vary the position of the rope so that it curves, makes right angles, or whatever shape the two players decide to challenge.

14   Circle Catch

Country: United States

Type: Ball

Players: 2

Age: 8–10

Equipment: 2 balls

FIGURE 8.14   . . . each
holding a ball.

Cooperative Elements: [x] Equality   [x] Trust
                        [x] Participation [ ] Success

How to Play

Players stand about six to seven feet apart, each holding a ball. On a signal from one of the players, both throw their ball toward the other. If both players catch the ball, they jump one step sideways in a counterclockwise direction, slightly turning as they do so in order to move in the shape of a circle with the diameter of six or seven feet. However, if the ball is dropped, no matter how far they have progressed around the imaginary circle, they must return to the starting position. The object of this game is to complete the circle.

15 Wall Catch

Country: England

Type: Ball

Players: 2

Age: 7–12

Equipment: 1 ball

FIGURE 8.15

FIGURE 8.16   If the other player catches it before . . .

Cooperative Elements: [x] Equality   [x] Trust
                        [x] Participation   [ ] Success

How to Play

The playing area is set up as shown in the drawing. The game starts with the pair standing behind the first line and one of the players throws the ball at the circle on the wall. If the other player catchs it before it touches the ground, they receive one point. Partners exchange positions after every throw. The game is played to ten points, then they move back to the next line and repeat the game until they have progressed to the line furthest from the wall.

16   Changing Positions

Country: Canada
Type: Manipulative
Players: 2
Age: 7–9
Equipment: Hoops and a
  balance bench

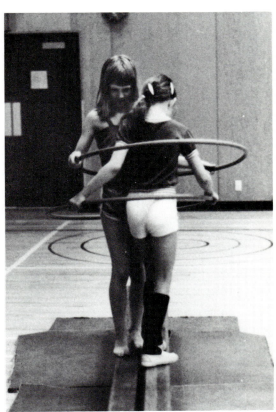

FIGURE 8.17   . . . pass
each other . . .

Cooperative Elements: [x] Equality   [x] Trust
                        [x] Participation   [ ] Success

How to Play

Two players begin at either end of a balance bench, each holding a hoop around themselves. They walk to the middle of the bench and without losing their balance, pass each other and continue on to the opposite end. Once this has been completed successfully, the complexity of the game is increased by the players choosing a modification to the activity, such as balancing a beanbag on their heads or changing the method of moving to a hop, slide, or other locomotor movement.

9

Games Involving Three Players and Stressing Participation and Success

   The first part of the following challenge is fairly structured; specifying one ball, one goal, and the action of dribbling with the feet. With these criteria it would be natural to invent a game that sets each player against the others with quick eliminations and an early declared winner. However, the requirements of the challenge stated in the second sentence insure that no player be eliminated and that each player reaps some success through participating in this game.

CHALLENGE: **"SEE IF YOUR GROUP OF THREE CAN MAKE UP A GAME WITH ONE BALL, ONE GOAL, AND DRIBBLE THE BALL WITH YOUR FEET. YOUR GAME MUST STRESS *PARTICIPATION* AND *SUCCESS*."**

1   Under the Leg

Country: China
Type: Ball
Players: 3
Age: 8–12
Equipment: 1 ball

FIGURE 9.1 . . . under her right and left leg . . .

Cooperative Elements: [x] Equality   [x] Trust
                         [x] Participation   [x] Success

How to Play

Players "A," "B," and "C" line up one behind the other with player "A" at the back of the line. Player "A" bounces the ball under her right and left leg then rolls it through player "B" 's legs. Player "B" repeats the same action, then rolls the ball through player "C" 's legs. When player "C" gets the ball, she bounces it under each leg, then places it on the ground and kicks it into a box located about ten feet away. Player "C" runs and retrieves the ball, takes it to the back of player "A," and starts to bounce the ball under her right then her left leg. After each player has had a turn, players may add new movements and rules.

2   Three Boys

Country: Botswana
Type: Ball
Players: 3
Age: 8–12
Equipment: 1 ball

FIGURE 9.2

Cooperative Elements: [x] Equality   [ ] Trust
                         [x] Participation   [x] Success

How to Play

A shallow hole or a box or hoop is used as a goal. Three players begin about twenty feet from the goal and begin to dribble and pass the ball to each other as they approach the goal. Any player can attempt to score providing he is at least six feet away from the goal. One point is awarded for each goal. The next player to attempt a goal must be one of the other two players. The game continues until the group has scored six points.

3   Goal

Country: Scotland
Type: Ball
Players: 3
Age: 8–12
Equipment: 1 soccer ball
  and 2 traffic cones

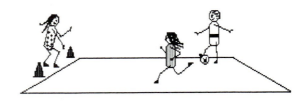

FIGURE 9.3   "Goal"

Cooperative Elements: [x] Equality   [ ] Trust
                        [x] Participation   [x] Success

How to Play

The "goal" is at one end of the playing area and "home" is at the other end. One player is "Goalkeeper" and the other two players start from "home," dribbling and passing the ball. The player who is in the act of dribbling may not score, however, when he feels his partner is in a good position to score, he shouts, "Goal," just before he passes the ball. The player receiving the pass must shoot at the goal without any further dribbling. If the ball goes into the goal, each of the two field players gets one point. If the ball misses or if the "Goalkeeper" prevents it from going in, the "Goalkeeper" rushes out and tries to tag one of the players. If the player is tagged before he can reach "home," they exchange positions. If the "Goalkeeper" is unsuccessful, he goes back into the goal and the game starts over.

4   Kickball

Country: Australia
Type: Ball
Players: 3
Age: 9–12
Equipment: 1 ball and
  1 bowling pin

FIGURE 9.4   . . . they race
to gain possession of . . .

Cooperative Elements: [x] Equality   [ ] Trust
                        [x] Participation   [ ] Success

How to Play

Three players stand behind a line about twenty feet away from a marker. On signal from the teacher, they race to gain possession of the ball. The player who touches the ball first is the "Shooter"; the other two run to protect the marker. The "Shooter" may dribble around until she is ready to shoot. She is allowed one shot on goal and if she hits the marker, she scores one point and is given a bonus shot. This is a free kick taken three yards away from the marker and while it is taken the other two players must stand beside her. If she hits the marker, she receives another point and the game starts again. If she misses, the game begins again with all three starting with a race toward the ball.

5   Circle Goal

Country: Jamaica
Type: Ball
Players: 3
Age: 9–12
Equipment: 1 soccer ball

FIGURE 9.5   Player "C" retrieves the ball . . .

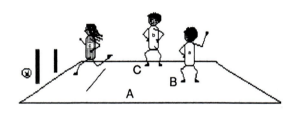

Cooperative Elements: [x] Equality   [ ] Trust
                        [x] Participation   [x] Success

How to Play

Arrange the playing area as shown in the illustration. Player "A" dribbles to "B" and remains there while player "B" dribbles to player "C" 's position. Player "B" remains and player "C" dribbles toward the goal and, without crossing the shooting line, attempts to score a goal. Player "C" retrieves her ball, passes it to player "B," then runs to take player "A" 's old position. Players "B" and "C" repeat the same movements after each player rotates one position counterclockwise.

6   Beanbag Smash

Country: South Africa
Type: Ball
Players: 3
Age: 8–10
Equipment: 1 ball, 3
  beanbags, and 3 traffic
  cones

FIGURE 9.6   The object of
the game . . .

Cooperative Elements: [x] Equality   [x] Trust
                        [x] Participation   [x] Success

How to Play

Three beanbags are placed on top of a traffic cone. Three players then make a triangle shape around the traffic cone. The object of the game is to use any part of their bodies except their hands to move the ball so that it knocks the beanbags off the traffic cone. Players must always remain at least three feet away from the traffic cone.

7   Snabbmal (Instant Goal)

Country: Sweden
Type: Ball
Players: 3
Age: 8–12
Equipment: 1 soccer ball

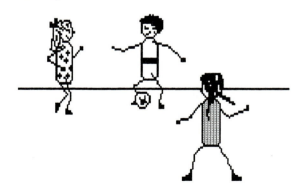

FIGURE 9.7   . . . must
dribble and pass the
ball . . .

Cooperative Elements: [x] Equality   [x] Trust
                        [x] Participation   [x] Success

How to Play

Three players begin dribbling and passing the ball to each other. Suddenly, player "A" moves away from the other two and spreads his legs to make a goal. The other two players must dribble and pass the ball at least two times before one of them tries to kick the ball between player "A"'s legs. The game continues with players "B" and "C" taking their turn at making a goal.

8   Claudia Berni

Country: Italy
Type: Ball
Players: 3
Age: 9–12
Equipment: 1 soccer ball
   and 1 hoop for each group
   of 3, and 8–12 traffic cones

FIGURE 9.8   If a group
touches either obstacle . . .

Cooperative Elements: [x] Equality   [x] Trust
                        [x] Participation   [x] Success

How to Play

Divide the class into groups of three and give each group one ball and one hoop. Two goals are marked on each end of the playground and the traffic cones are scattered throughout the playing area. Each group begins on one end line standing inside their hoop and holding it about waist high. The object of this game is for each group to dribble their ball around two traffic cones as they move toward the opposite end, then kick the ball and hit the post. If a group touches a traffic cone they must pick up their ball, walk back to the starting line, and try again. No scores are kept and the membership of each group is changed every few minutes.

9   Arquitos (Little Arches)

Country: Peru
Type: Ball
Players: 3
Age: 8–12
Equipment: 1 soccer ball

FIGURE 9.9   If successful, he scores one point . . .

Cooperative Elements: [x] Equality   [x] Trust
                          [x] Participation   [x] Success

How to Play

Two players stand about six feet apart with their legs apart, facing the third player. The third player begins dribbling the ball toward the first player, and, when ready, attempts to kick the ball through the first player's legs. If successful he scores one point and tries to score another goal with the second player. Players with their legs apart may use their hands to prevent the ball from going through their legs. If a player stops the ball, he changes positions with the third player and the game starts over. If a player scores the first two goals, he turns around with the ball and while the other two players are facing away from him, tries to kick the ball so that it rolls through both player's legs. If successful, he gets two points for his double goal. However, if the ball only goes through one player's legs, he does not get a point and exchanges positions with the front player.

10   ABC Dribble

Country: England
Type: Ball
Players: 3
Age: 9–12
Equipment: 1 soccer ball
and 3 traffic cones

FIGURE 9.10   Player "A" dribbles around the traffic cones . . .

Cooperative Elements: [x] Equality   [ ] Trust
[x] Participation   [x] Success

How to Play

Arrange players as shown in the diagram. Player "A" dribbles around the three traffic cones, shoots for a goal, then takes player "B" 's position. If "B" stops the ball, she moves to player "A" 's position and takes her turn. If player "B" fails to stop the ball, player "C" picks it up and runs to take player "A" 's starting position. Player "B" drops back to player "C" 's position and player "A" becomes the new goalkeeper. No score is kept with all players moving as fast as possible from one position to the next.

11   Hoop Soccer

Country: Australia
Type: Ball
Players: 3
Age: 8–12
Equipment: 1 soccer ball,
1 hoop, and 1 basket

FIGURE 9.11

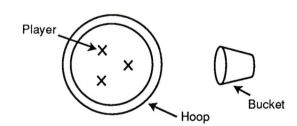

Cooperative Elements: [x] Equality   [x] Trust
[x] Participation   [x] Success

How to Play

Three players stand inside a hoop and hold it about waist high. Once inside the hoop, the players begin to dribble the ball toward the overturned basket. When they reach shooting distance, one player attempts to score a goal. They retrieve the ball and return to the starting line and start a new game. On the second attempt, a new player must attempt to shoot a goal. This procedure is followed on each successive attempt on the goal.

Note: Players found the most efficient way to dribble the ball was to rotate their positions within the hoop while moving toward the target. This movement allowed each player to touch the ball during the dribbling part of the game.

12 Roll the Ball Home

Country: Wales

Type: Ball

Players: 3

Age: 9–12

Equipment: 1 soccer ball
and 1 goal

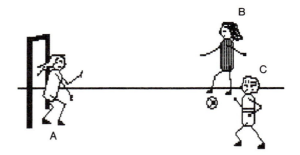

FIGURE 9.12 Players "B" and "C" start dribbling . . .

Cooperative Elements: [x] Equality   [ ] Trust
                        [x] Participation   [ ] Success

How to Play

Player "A" begins in goal and players "B" and "C" start about twenty feet away from the goal. Players "B" and "C" start dribbling and passing the ball and as they approach player "A" they try to dribble past her. They cannot kick the ball past player "A." If a goal is scored, players "B" and "C" try again. If player "A" touches the ball before it is dribbled through the goal, she changes position with the player who was dribbling the ball at the moment the ball was touched.

13   Hit the Hoop

Country: Japan
Type: Ball
Players: 3
Age: 8–12
Equipment: 1 ball and
    1 hoop

FIGURE 9.13   If player "B"
intercepts the ball . . .

Cooperative Elements: [x] Equality   [ ] Trust
                         [x] Participation   [ ] Success

How to Play

Player "A" stands and holds a hoop just off the ground. Player "C" starts with a ball about thirty feet away from player "A" and player "B" stands between players "A" and "C." Player "C" begins to dribble the ball toward player "A" and as he approaches player "B," tries to keep him from stealing the ball. If player "B" intercepts the ball, he tries to dribble it as well as to keep player "C" from regaining possession of it. If player "C" can keep possession of the ball and can kick it through the hoop, he scores one point and gets another turn. If he fails to score a point, he changes places with player "A" and the game starts over, with player "B" starting to dribble the ball forward.

14   Fire Fighter's Rescue

Country: Canada
Type: Ball
Players: 3
Age: 9–12
Equipment: 1 ball and
  1 basket

FIGURE 9.14   . . . then
the fire fighters carry her
back . . .

FIGURE 9.15

Cooperative Elements: [x] Equality   [x] Trust
                        [x] Participation   [x] Success

How to Play

There are three players. Two form a fire fighter's chair with their arms crossed and their hands joined, and the third player sits on their hands. A basket is placed on one side of the gymnasium as the starting point. When ready, the two fire fighters carry the third player and begin to dribble and pass the ball toward the opposite side of the gymnasium. When they reach the other side, the third player picks up the ball between her feet, then the fire fighters carry her back to the basket. Rotate position and repeat the game.

15   Blind Horse

Country: Argentina
Type: Ball
Players: 3
Age: 8–12
Equipment: 1 ball, 4 sticks,
   and 2 traffic cones

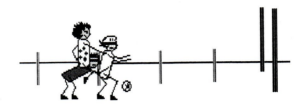

FIGURE 9.16   . . . and
player "C" guides them . . .

Cooperative Elements: [x] Equality   [x] Trust
                        [x] Participation   [x] Success

How to Play

Arrange the playing area as shown in the illustration. Player "A" bends forward and puts his arms around player "B" 's waist. Player "C" then sits on player "A" 's back. Players "A" and "B" keep their eyes closed and player "C" guides them to move the ball around the four sticks and through the goal. Players change positions after each goal and begin at the starting line.

16   Soap Box Soccer

Country: United States
Type: Ball
Players: 3
Age: 9–12
Equipment: 1 soccer ball
   and 1 basket

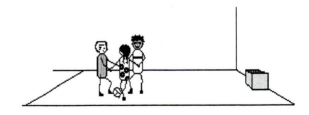

FIGURE 9.17   They must
keep the ball inside . . .

Cooperative Elements: [x] Equality   [x] Trust
                        [x] Participation   [x] Success

How to Play

A soccer ball is placed on the starting line. Three players hold hands and form a triangle around the ball. They must keep the ball inside the triangle and dribble the ball to the basket. When they reach the basket, each player can use one foot to help lift the ball into the basket. Repeat the game with players rotating clockwise as they dribble the ball toward the basket.

17   Drierfubball

Country: Germany
Type: Ball
Players: 3
Age: 9–12
Equipment: 1 soccer ball
and 2 traffic cones

FIGURE 9.18   . . . and
throws the ball with a high
arc . . .

Cooperative Elements: [x] Equality   [ ] Trust
[x] Participation   [ ] Success

How to Play

Player "A" is the goalkeeper and throws the ball with a high arc into the playing area. Players "B" and "C" try to gain possession of the ball and score a goal. Players may shoot from either side of the goal. If a player scores a goal, the other player becomes the new goalkeeper and the game starts over.

18   Soccer Circuit

Country: New Zealand
Type: Ball
Players: 3
Age: 9–12
Equipment: 1 ball and
2 traffic cones

FIGURE 9.19   Player "A"
dribbles the ball around . . .

Cooperative Elements: [x] Equality   [x] Trust
[x] Participation   [ ] Success

How to Play

Arrange players as shown in the illustration. Player "A" dribbles the ball around the goal and when he is at the side of the goal, he passes the ball to player "B." As player "B" receives the ball and attempts to score a goal, player "A" moves behind the goal to stop the ball if it gets past player "C." After player "B" takes his turn, he takes player "A" 's original position, player "C" becomes the new shooter, and player "A" becomes the goalkeeper. Repeat game and rotate playing positions.

19   **Triple Dribble**

Country: India
Type: Ball
Players: 3
Age: 9–12
Equipment: 1 ball and
   2 traffic cones

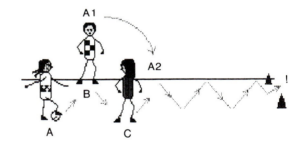

FIGURE 9.20   Player "A"
dribbles the ball to . . .

Cooperative Elements:	[x] Equality	[ ] Trust
	[x] Participation	[x] Success

How to Play

Arrange players as shown in the illustration. Player "A" dribbles the ball to player "B." Player "B" then dribbles it to player "C," while player "A" moves to a new position. Player "C" now dribbles to player "A" while player "B" moves to a new position. Continue rotation until one player can dribble the ball through the goal. Repeat game from the original starting position.

10

Games Involving the Whole Class and Stressing Participation and Equality

This was one of the most difficult challenges of the project. As mentioned in Chapter 6, making up a game for the whole class is a major task for young children. In this challenge, the complexity of the task is increased by requiring the players to use all available space and to play without any equipment. The additional requirement of including the elements of participation and equality added even more to the complexity of the task and made this a "real challenge" for the children.

The games that resulted ranged from running and tag activities to group statues that represented geometrical shapes or animals that moved in a variety of ways and directions. They show that children interpret each challenge in their own unique way, and that each group draws upon their inherent creative abilities to meet the challenge.

CHALLENGE: "SEE IF YOU CAN MAKE UP A GAME FOR THE WHOLE CLASS, USING ALL THE AVAILABLE SPACE, AND NO EQUIPMENT. YOUR GAME MUST STRESS *PARTICIPATION* AND *EQUALITY*."

1   Zumkha

Country: India
Type: Running
Players: Class
Age: 7–10
Equipment: None

FIGURE 10.1   "Six"

Cooperative Elements: [x] Equality   [ ] Trust
                        [x] Participation   [x] Success

How to Play

   The class begins in a large circle facing counterclockwise. The teacher stands in the middle and signals the class to walk, run, or perform any other type of locomotor movement. As the players are moving, the teacher calls out a number, such as "Five," signaling all players to get into groups of five. Those players who fail to get into groups according to the called number, must say a rhyme or perform a trick before the game begins again. The game always starts with all players in a circle formation.

2   Step on My Shadow

Country: Botswana
Type: Tag
Players: Class
Age: 8–10
Equipment: None

FIGURE 10.2   . . . each player tries to step on . . .

Cooperative Elements: [x] Equality   [ ] Trust
                        [x] Participation   [ ] Success

How to Play

Mark off a playing area of about ten to fifteen square yards and have class scatter within the area. On signal from the teacher, each player tries to step on as many other players' shadows as possible while keeping other players from stepping on his own shadow.

3   Horses in the Corral

Country: Barbados
Type: Tag
Players: Class
Age: 8–12
Equipment: None

FIGURE 10.3   On signal from the teacher . . .

Cooperative Elements: [x] Equality   [ ] Trust
                          [x] Participation   [ ] Success

How to Play

Mark off a playing area about ten by thirty yards and draw a circle (corral) in the middle of the playing area. Divide class into two equal groups. To start the game, Group A is designated as the "Cowboys" and must start from inside the corral. Group B, the "Horses," scatter in the playing area. On signal from the teacher, "Horses" may run anywhere within the playing area and "Cowboys" try to tag as many "Horses" as they can within a time period of thirty seconds. When a "Horse" is tagged she must run to the corral, run around it once, then return to the playing area. Each group takes a turn at being the "Cowboys." The team with the largest number of "Horses" tagged, is the winner.

4   Robots

Country: Germany
Type: Manipulative
Players: 3 per group
Age: 8–12
Equipment: None

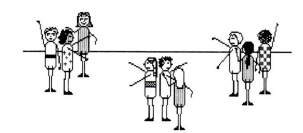

FIGURE 10.4   . . . by
slightly touching them . . .

Cooperative Elements: [x] Equality   [x] Trust
                        [x] Participation   [x] Success

How to Play

Arrange class into groups of three. Two players are the "Robots," the other player is the "Engineer" who steers the robots. The "Robots" can only move forward and make right-angled turns. To start, "Robots" stand back-to-back, then the engineer begins to move the robots by slightly touching them on their right shoulders (right-angled turn), left shoulders (left-angled turn), or head (straight ahead one step). The task of the "Engineer" is to move the "Robots" so they face each other, stand side by side, or face one behind the other. Players change positions after the "Robots" are facing whatever position they agreed upon. The next game can be played with the "Robots" keeping their eyes closed.

5   Tallia

Country: Greece
Type: Manipulative
Players: 12
Age: 8–12
Equipment: None

FIGURE 10.5   . . . climb
on their backs . . .

Cooperative Elements: [x] Equality   [x] Trust
                        [x] Participation   [x] Success

How to Play

Arrange class into groups of twelve players. One-half of each group forms a line and the first player holds on to a tree or another stable object. Each player then places his head between the legs of the player directly in front of him. The remaining six players climb on their backs and stay there until the leader counts to a certain number. If all six players stay on for the full count, they score one point. If any player touches the ground during the counting, they start over. Reverse rolls and repeat the game.

6   Animals

Country: New Zealand
Type: Manipulative
Players: Class
Age: 9–12
Equipment: None

FIGURE 10.6   . . . has two heads, twelve legs, and one tail.

Cooperative Elements: [x] Equality   [x] Trust
                         [x] Participation   [x] Success

How to Play

Divide class into two or three groups of ten to twelve players in each group. The teacher describes an imaginary animal. The imaginary animal might be something like, . . . "It has two heads, twelve legs, and one tail." Each group then decides how they will create and illustrate this animal. One additional rule is added—the animal must move ten yards.

7   Emergency

Country: Canada
Type: Manipulative
Players: Class
Age: 8–12
Equipment: None

FIGURE 10.7   If a player is tagged, she must . . .

FIGURE 10.8

Cooperative Elements: [x] Equality   [x] Trust
                         [x] Participation   [ ] Success

How to Play

Two players are chosen to be "It" (Forces of Evil) and stand in the middle of the playing area. All other players are the "Para-Medics," and stand on the end line ("hospital zone"). "It" calls "Emergency!" which signals everyone to leave the "hospital zone" and run to the opposite end. The two "It" players try to tag as many "Para-Medics" as possible before they reach the opposite end. If a player is tagged, she must lie down and pretend she is injured. In order for an injured player to be rescued, four players must run and touch the injured player before being tagged. As soon as four untagged players have touched the injured player, they cannot be tagged until they have carried the injured player across the end line and reentered the playing area. After two or three minutes, change the "It" players and start the game over.

8   Geometry Class

Country: Argentina
Type: Manipulative
Players: Class
Age: 8–12
Equipment: None

FIGURE 10.9   Team "A" forms the geometrical shape . . .

Cooperative Elements: [x] Equality   [ ] Trust
                         [x] Participation   [x] Success

How to Play

The class is divided into two teams. Each team writes the name of five different geometrical shapes on separate pieces of paper, then places them face down in the middle of the playing area. One player from team "A" selects one of the ten pieces of paper, reads the name of the shape to himself, then whispers it to his teammates. Team "A" forms the geometrical shape then team "B" tries to guess its name. Teams exchange positions after each shape is formed and the winner is the team that correctly guesses the highest number of geometrical shapes.

9   Frog, Jump, and Slide

Country: South Africa

Type: Manipulative

Players: 5–6 per group

Age: 8–12

Equipment: None

FIGURE 10.10   . . . last person starts crawling . . .

FIGURE 10.11   . . . and each child leapfrogs over . . .

FIGURE 10.12   . . . leads her team around a full circle . . .

Cooperative Elements: [x] Equality   [x] Trust
                        [x] Participation   [x] Success

How to Play

Each group of five or six players begins standing in a row, one behind the other with their legs apart. The last person starts crawling through the legs. As soon as she has passed two players, the next person begins and so on until the last child has crawled through the group. Next, the players spread apart but remain in a row and each child leapfrogs over every other member of the team. Finally, the front player leads her team around a full circle and back to the starting position. Last player moves to the front of the line and repeats the game. Continue game until players are back in their original positions.

10   Alley Tag

Country: Japan
Type: Tag
Players: Class
Age: 8–12
Equipment: None

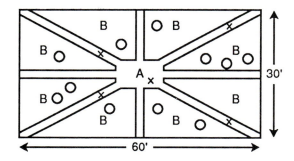

FIGURE 10.13   Alley Tag

FIGURE 10.14   Players must leap over alleys.

Cooperative Elements: [x] Equality   [ ] Trust
                          [x] Participation   [x] Success

How to Play

Arrange the playing area as shown in the diagram. Five players are chosen to be "It" and may move anywhere within area A. All remaining players must stay within the space designated as area B. On signal from the teacher, the players in area B run clockwise around the playing area and try to get back to their starting positions without being tagged. Players must not touch alleys but may cross them with a leap. If a player is tagged or touches an alley, he joins the taggers in area A. As soon as the taggers have tagged ten players, five new "It" players are chosen by the teacher and the game continues.

11   Divisible Snake

Country: Luxembourg
Type: Tag
Players: Class
Age: 7–10
Equipment: None

FIGURE 10.15   . . . and tag a fourth player.

Cooperative Elements: [x] Equality   [ ] Trust
                          [x] Participation   [ ] Success

How to Play

Two children are chosen to be the first snake and hold hands while the remainder of the class scatters in the playing area. On signal from the teacher, the snake tries to tag other players. When a player is tagged he must hold on to one of the taggers and they continue to try and tag a fourth player. Once a fourth player is tagged, the group divides into two and the game continues. The last two players to be caught become the new snake and the game starts over.

12 Search for the Name

Country: United States
Type: Manipulative
Players: Class
Age: 8–10
Equipment: None

FIGURE 10.16 . . . begins to feel the player's face . . .

Cooperative Elements: [x] Equality   [x] Trust
                          [x] Participation   [ ] Success

How to Play

Arrange the class into a circle formation, and place one player ("It") in the middle. "It" keeps his eyes closed while the circle players move clockwise. When "It" feels ready, he calls "Stop," then walks forward to touch a circle player. "It" begins to feel the player's face and arms, etc., and tries to guess the name of the person he is touching. If he guesses correctly, they exchange positions, and if wrong, he tries another player.

13   North, South, East, West

Country: England
Type: Manipulative
Players: Class
Age: 8–10
Equipment: None

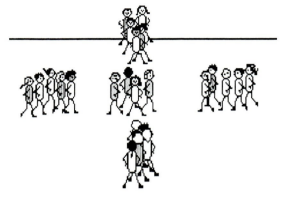

FIGURE 10.17   . . . divide
into four equal groups . . .

Cooperative Elements: [x] Equality   [ ] Trust
                        [x] Participation   [ ] Success

How to Play

Four children are chosen to be "It" and stand in the middle of the playing area. The remainder of the class divides into four equal groups and stand in their group about four yards away from each compass point. The game begins with the teacher saying "North, South, East, West," and waits about ten seconds to allow the four players in the middle to look around to see where every player in each group is located. After the ten seconds have elapsed, all four players must close their eyes for another ten seconds. During this time, all players within each group may change their position to another group. The teacher calls, "Open your eyes" and allows the North player to say where everyone on her compass point has come from. If she is correct she remains in her position. The first player that she does not identify correctly changes positions with her. All other players in the middle complete their turn before the game starts again.

14   Mic Mac Relay

Country: France
Type: Running
Players: Class
Age: 9–12
Equipment: None

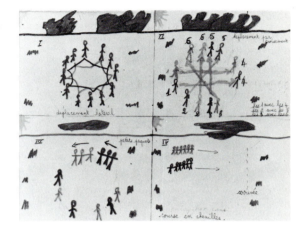

FIGURE 10.18

Cooperative Elements: [x] Equality   [ ] Trust
                        [x] Participation   [x] Success

How to Play

Arrange the class into groups of twelve players and number players as shown in the diagram. The game is played in the following four phases and the team that completes all four phases first wins the game. On signal from the teacher start with phase number one and continue to number four.

Phase Number One: Sideways Run: One's run to two's, two's to three's, and so on until all players are back in their original positions.

Phase Number Two: Criss-Cross Exchange: Pair one and four exchange positions, followed by two and five, then three and six. (Note an error in the children's drawing.)

Phase Number Three: Little Bunches: Pair number one's run around the circle, pick up pair number two's, continue running around, pick up number three's, four's, five's, and sixes in the same fashion.

Phase Number Four: Caterpillar Race: As soon as pair sixes have been grabbed, they all squat down, hold each other's waists, and caterpillar walk to the finish line. If the line breaks, players must return to the original position and start again.

15   Carbonales, Cardenales, Carpinteros

Country: Peru
Type: Tag
Players: Class
Age: 8–12
Equipment: None

FIGURE 10.19   The leader is called ''Cardenale'' . . .

FIGURE 10.20
. . . players are called ''Carbonales'' . . .

Cooperative Elements: [x] Equality   [ ] Trust
                        [x] Participation   [x] Success

How to Play

The leader is called "Cardenale" and stands on the end line. All other players are called "Carbonales" and stand behind the starting line. The space between the "Carbonales" and the "Cardenale" is known as "Carpinteros." The leader calls out, "Cardenales!" and all players begin to run toward the opposite end. As they are running, the leader may call out, "Carpinteros!" which means all players must stop; or if "Cardenale" calls this out when they are already stopped they must remain motionless. If he calls out, "Carbonales!" players must move backwards. Any player who commits an error must return to the starting line. The first player to cross "Carbonale's" line takes his place and the game starts over.

16   Humpy Bumpy Caterpillars

Country: Australia
Type: Manipulative
Players: Class
Age: 9–12
Equipment: None

FIGURE 10.21
. . . longest walking
caterpillar . . .

Cooperative Elements: [x] Equality   [x] Trust
                        [x] Participation   [x] Success

How to Play

The whole class attempts to make the longest walking caterpillar by joining together as follows. (1) One child crouches on her hands and knees. (2) The second child stretches over the top of the first child so that her hands and feet are in contact with the floor. (3) The third child holds onto the first child's ankles and her own knees touch the floor. (4) The fourth child assumes the same position as number two. (5) Once the class has assembled the caterpillar, they try to move forward without breaking apart.

11

Games from a Teacher's Special Challenge

By the time the teachers and children reached this phase of the project, they were used to handling a variety of challenges with ease and effectiveness. In Chapter 7 teachers were given their first opportunity to create and present their own challenge to their class. They showed a great deal of ingenuity in preparing their challenges to cope with the unique conditions relating to the cultural and physical features of their local area. A similar opportunity was given in this chapter. The challenge in this case included one or more elements of a cooperative game. This requirement set the stage for the type of game that would be created. As expected, the teachers used their creative talents in designing their challenges and the children continued to demonstrate their understanding of this process as illustrated in the following games.

NOTE TO TEACHERS: "MAKE UP YOUR OWN CHALLENGE. YOU MAY SELECT ANY NUMBER OF PLAYERS, AS WELL AS IMPOSE YOUR OWN LIMITATIONS WITH RESPECT TO EQUIPMENT, SKILLS, AND RULES. ALSO, YOUR CHALLENGE MAY STRESS ONE OR ALL THE ELEMENTS OF A COOPERATIVE GAME."

1   KHO

Country: India
Type: Tag
Players: Class
Age: 8–12
Equipment: None

FIGURE 11.1   . . . and the outside circle player becomes the . . .

Cooperative Elements: [x] Equality   [ ] Trust
                        [x] Participation   [ ] Success

Teacher's Challenge: "Make up a tag game for the whole class but do
                       not use any equipment."

How to Play

Arrange the class in a double circle, one behind the other and facing the
center of the circle. One player is designated as the "Chaser" and another
as the "Runner." On the signal, "Go!" the "Chaser" tries to tag the "Runner"
who runs in and out of the circle players. When the "Runner" stands in
front of an inside circle player, she calls out "KHO," and the outside circle
player becomes the new "Runner." If a "Runner" is tagged before she can
stand in front of a circle player, she must change positions with the "Chaser."

2   Bomb in the Box

Country: England
Type: Manipulative
Players: 6
Age: 8–12
Equipment: 1 hoop and
   1 skip rope

FIGURE 11.2

Cooperative Elements: [x] Equality   [x] Trust
                        [x] Participation   [x] Success

Teacher's Challenge: "Make up a game that has six players. You must
                       use a hoop and a skipping rope. Your game must
                       have equal turns, everyone must take part, and you
                       must use trust in your game."

How to Play

Players line up as shown in the drawing. Number one places her hoop
on her foot. Without using her hands she passes it "footwise" to player
number two. Each player repeats this movement until the hoop reaches
player number four. Player number four must now lift the hoop over the

rope without using her hands, then changes positions with player number six. Player number six picks up the hoop with his foot, returns to the front of the line, and passes the hoop to player number two. Continue the rotation until everyone has had a turn.

3   Pirates

Country: Germany
Type: Ball
Players: Class
Age: 8–12
Equipment: 15–20 hoops
    and 6–8 balls

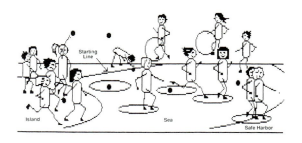

FIGURE 11.3   One half of the class are ''Pirates'' . . .

Cooperative Elements: [x] Equality   [ ] Trust
                        [x] Participation   [ ] Success

Teacher's Challenge: ''See if you can make up a game for the whole class using small utility or nerf balls. Your game must stress participation and success.''

How to Play

The playing area is divided into an ''Island,'' a ''Safe Harbor,'' and the ''Sea,'' as shown in the illustration. One half of the class are ''Pirates'' and must stay in the island area. The other half are ''Traders'' and must move their ships (hoops) from the starting line across the sea, by only using their feet, to the safe harbor. If a ''Pirate'' throws the ball and hits the hoop or lands inside it, the ship sinks. However, the ''Trader'' inside a sinking ship may jump to the nearest ship and help move it to the ''Safe Harbor.'' The sinking ''Trader'' is allowed only one jump to reach the other ship, hence, may have to wait for another ''Trader'' to move close to him. When this ship reaches the safe harbor, the pair separates and the ''Trader'' who was sunk returns to his ship and continues his voyage. The other ''Trader'' must pick up his ship and walk back to the starting line around the outside of the playing area and begin again. If a ''Pirate'' throws a ball which does not hit a ship, he waits until it has stopped moving and then touches another ''Pirate'' to go and retrieve the ball. When the retrieving ''Pirate'' picks up a ball, he must move outside the playing area and run back to his island before he takes his turn to throw the ball. The game ends after a time limit or if all the ships are sunk at the same time and there are no seaworthy ships to rescue the sinking ''Traders.''

4   Jump Ball

Country: Botswana
Type: Ball
Players: 3
Age: 8–10
Equipment: 1 ball

FIGURE 11.4   Player "A" bounces the ball to player "C" . . .

Cooperative Elements: [x] Equality   [ ] Trust
                                   [x] Participation   [x] Success

Teacher's Challenge: "Try and make up a game with three players, one ball, a bounce, and a catch."

How to Play

   Three players begin in a straight line with player "A" holding the ball. Player "A" bounces the ball to player "C" then changes positions with player "B." Player "C" bounces the ball to player "B" and changes positions with player "A." Continue rotation until someone commits an error, then start the game over.

5   Blind Flight

Country: Luxembourg
Type: Manipulative
Players: 10
Age: 10–12
Equipment: 1 rope and
   4 traffic cones

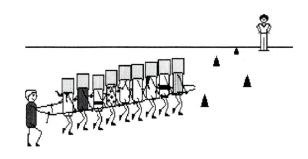

FIGURE 11.5   The guide tries to lead . . .

Cooperative Elements: [x] Equality   [x] Trust
                                   [x] Participation   [x] Success

Teacher's Challenge: "See if you can make up a game for ten players, using all the available space and equipment. Your game must stress equality, participation, success, and trust."

How to Play

The first nine players hold the rope at the sides of their bodies then place a paper bag over their heads. The last player (guide) arranges the four traffic cones, comes back to his group, and teaches them three nonverbal commands. These are (1) "Pull right," means front player turns right, (2) "Pull left," means front player turns left, (3) "Pull on both," means front player moves straight ahead. The guide then tries to lead the group to the first traffic cone. When the front player touches the first traffic cone, he replaces the cone in another spot then exchanges positions with the guide. The old guide takes the paper bag and moves to the back of the group to become the last player. The group continues to the next cone, changes players, and continues this pattern to the last player.

6 Electric Gate

Country: China
Type: Tag
Players: Class
Age: 9–12
Equipment: None

FIGURE 11.6   . . . players from team "A" run out . . .

Cooperative Elements: [x] Equality   [ ] Trust
                        [x] Participation   [ ] Success

Teacher's Challenge: "See if you can make up a game for the whole group using all the available space and no equipment. Your game must stress equality and participation."

How to Play

Divide the class into two equal teams and place each team on opposite lines. Two basketball standards are used as the "Electric Gates." On signal from the teacher, players from team "A" run out and try to touch team "B" 's gate before getting tagged by a team "B" player. If any player on team "A" is tagged, he must remain in a "frozen" position. He can be "unfrozen" by another player of his own team touching him, providing she "unfreezes" her teammate before she is tagged by the other team. The game continues until a player from team "A" touches the opponent's "electric gate," or when all members of team "A" are frozen. The game starts over with members of team "B" running out to touch team "A" 's "Electric Gate."

7   Mat Pull

Country: Japan
Type: Manipulative
Players: Class
Age: 8–12
Equipment: Mats

FIGURE 11.7   . . . to pull as many players off . . .

Cooperative Elements: [x] Equality   [x] Trust
                         [x] Participation   [ ] Success

Teacher's Challenge: "Can you make up a game for the whole class using mats? Your game must stress participation and equality."

How to Play

   Divide the class into two equal teams. Team "A" stands on the mat and team "B" stands around the mat. The object of the game is for the players on team "B" to pull as many team "A" players as they can off the mat. Players on the mat may help each other by holding teammates; however, hitting, striking, or any other harmful movements are not permitted. Once a player is pulled off the mat, he must stay clear of the mat until the game is completed. After a set time limit, the teams exchange positions. The team with the largest number remaining on the mat wins the game.

8   Hoop Tag

Country: Australia
Type: Manipulative
Players: 6
Age: 8–12
Equipment: 1 tennis ball and
   1 hoop

FIGURE 11.8   If "It" can place the hoop . . .

Cooperative Elements: [x] Equality   [ ] Trust
                        [x] Participation   [ ] Success

Teacher's Challenge: "Your game has six players, one small ball, one
                        hoop, a throw, and a catch. Your game must also
                        stress participation of all players throughout the
                        game."

How to Play

One player is chosen to be "It" and is given a hoop. The other players
may move anywhere within the designated playing area and throw the ball
back and forth to each other. If the ball is not caught in the air or after one
bounce, the player who commits the error changes positions with "It." If
the player throwing the ball throws a poor pass, she changes positions with
"It." If "It" can place the hoop over a player who has possession of the
ball, they exchange positions.

9   Copy Us

Country: Jamaica
Type: Manipulative
Players: 12
Age: 7–9
Equipment: None

FIGURE 11.9   . . . to
demonstrate their
original . . .

Cooperative Elements: [x] Equality   [ ] Trust
                        [x] Participation   [x] Success

Teacher's Challenge: "Design a game using twelve players. Each player
                        picks a partner then everyone forms a circle. Each
                        pair comes to the center of the circle and performs
                        an activity and everyone must copy their
                        movement."

How to Play

Children are allowed to choose their partners then everyone forms a circle. Each pair takes their turn to demonstrate their original movement. As new pairs come to the center, they cannot repeat the activity of any previous couple.

10   Bildaren (Bad Car Driver)

Country: Sweden
Type: Tag
Players: Class
Age: 9–12
Equipment: 1 large mat

FIGURE 11.10   . . . and may carry the injured player . . .

Cooperative Elements: [x] Equality   [x] Trust
                        [x] Participation   [ ] Success

Teacher's Challenge: "Plan a game that will involve the whole class. It must stress everyone is active. Somewhere in your game one player must place trust in another player."

How to Play

One large mat (hospital) is placed in the center of the floor. One player is selected to be the "Bildaren," who tries to tag other players. If a player is tagged (car accident), he must lie down on the floor and become an injured person. Any four players may run to the hospital mat, and if not tagged before they reach it, they are safe. They are then immune and may carry the injured player back to the hospital mat where he is then free to join the game again and the rescuers are no longer immune. When the "Bildaren" has four injured players on the floor, he changes places with the first person tagged.

11   Captain's Ride

Country: Argentina
Type: Manipulative
Players: 7–8
Age: 10–12
Equipment: 2 long ropes and
  an old tire

FIGURE 11.11   . . . "The
Captain" balances on the
tire . . .

Cooperative Elements: [x] Equality   [x] Trust
                        [x] Participation   [x] Success

Teacher's Challenge: "Imagine a game with seven or eight players,
                       using two ropes, an old tire, or any other available
                       equipment."

How to Play

Players tie two long ropes to an old tire. Three players hold on to each
rope. The seventh player, "The Captain," balances on the tire while the
"Crew" of six drag the tire twenty to thirty yards along the ground. Both
the "Crew" and "Captain" attempt a good ride without the "Captain" falling
off the tire. Each player rotates to the "Captain's" position.

12   Hog's Ball

Country: South Africa
Type: Ball
Players: 10 per team
Age: 8–12
Equipment: 4 hoops and
  2 balls

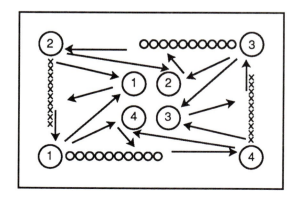

FIGURE 11.12   "Hog's
Ball"

FIGURE 11.13
. . . returns and stands three
yards away . . .

Cooperative Elements: [x] Equality   [ ] Trust
                        [x] Participation   [x] Success

Teacher's Challenge: "Invent a game for two teams of five players each.
                        Each player must contribute equally to the success
                        of the game."

How to Play

Arrange the playing area as shown in the diagram. Player number one
from each team runs and gets the ball from the center of the circle, returns
and stands three yards away from her team, then passes the ball to each
player on her team. From here, the player runs to her end line and bounces
the ball in her team's hoop, then returns to the center and places the ball
in her team's other hoop. She then runs and tags player number two who
repeats the same movements. The first team to complete the relay wins the
game.

13   Five and Ten Ball

Country: Belgium
Type: Ball
Players: 10
Age: 9–12
Equipment: 1 beanbag

FIGURE 11.14   . . . and
throw the beanbag to
number . . .

Cooperative Elements: [x] Equality   [ ] Trust
                       [x] Participation   [ ] Success

Teacher's Challenge: "See if your group of ten can invent a new game
                       that is played in a circle formation and uses a
                       beanbag. The game must stress participation and
                       trust."

How to Play

All ten players sit in a circle. One player starts to pass the beanbag and
calls himself number one. The next child takes the beanbag and calls himself number two, and so on until the last number is called. When number
ten calls out his number he has to stand up and throw the beanbag to
number five. Number five stands up and begins to run around the circle to
try and tag number ten. When number ten finally gets touched, they sit
down at any place in the circle, and number ten starts counting again from
number one and passing the beanbag.

14   Interceptor

Country: New Zealand
Type: Ball
Players: 8
Age: 9–12
Equipment: 1 soccer ball

FIGURE 11.15   Player
number one starts . . .

Cooperative Elements: [x] Equality   [ ] Trust
                       [x] Participation   [x] Success

Teacher's Challenge: "Make up a game with eight players and one
                       soccer ball. You must use a dribble, trap, and pass
                       in your game. The game must also have the
                       elements of equality and participation."

How to Play

Players one to seven scatter anywhere in the playing area. Player number
one starts dribbling the ball from one end of the field to the opposite end.
He must pass the ball to each player as he moves toward the opposite end,
turns around, and repeats the same action until he reaches player number
two. Players one and two exchange positions and player two dribbles the
ball to the starting line, then begins his turn. Repeat game for every player.

15   Grasshopper

Country: Peru
Type: Manipulative
Players: Class
Age: 7–10
Equipment: Small object

FIGURE 11.16   . . . the "Grasshopper" and stands inside . . .

Cooperative Elements: [x] Equality   [x] Trust
                         [x] Participation   [ ] Success

Teacher's Challenge: "Could you design a cooperative game that includes your friend and any object? You must take into account that the two of you should do the same thing and somehow trust each other."

How to Play

Arrange players in pairs and form a large circle with partners standing side by side. One pair is chosen to be the "Grasshopper" and stands inside the circle, back to back, elbows locked, and balancing a small object between their shoulders. They must stay about three feet away from the circle players. As the circle players begin to clap their hands, the two inside players must start jumping clockwise around the circle, keeping their elbows locked, balancing the object between their shoulders, and keeping time to the rhythm of the children's clapping. Circle players may speed up or slow down the speed of their clapping. If the "Grasshopper" drops the object, they change places with the couple closest to them and the game begins again. If the "Grasshopper" makes it around the circle without dropping the object, they change places with the next pair.

16   Balloon Battle

Country: United States
Type: Ball
Players: Class
Age: 8–12
Equipment: 1 balloon or
  beach ball

FIGURE 11.17   . . . to bat
the balloon to the . . .

Cooperative Elements: [x] Equality   [ ] Trust
                        [x] Participation   [x] Success

Teacher's Challenge: "Can you make up a game using all the available
                       space, a balloon, and the whole class? The game
                       must stress equality, participation, and trust."

How to Play

The class is divided in two equal teams and scattered in the playing area. From this position, players may move anywhere so long as they keep their behinds on the floor. The object of the game is to bat the balloon to the opponent's wall. After each goal is scored, the game is restarted by the teacher who stands on the sidelines in the middle of the playing area, facing away from the class. She then tosses the balloon backwards over her head.

17   Moving Musical Hoops

Country: Canada
Type: Manipulative
Players: Class
Age: 8–12
Equipment: Class set of
   hoops

FIGURE 11.18   . . . and
begins to run anywhere . . .

FIGURE 11.19   "Three"

Cooperative Elements: [x] Equality   [x] Trust
                        [x] Participation   [x] Success

Teacher's Challenge: "Try and invent a game where no player is
                      eliminated and every player is successful."

How to Play

Every player starts inside his hoop and begins to run anywhere within
the playing area. As the players are running, the teacher calls out "two"
and all players must link up in twos and keep running. The game continues
with the teacher calling out "three," "four," etc., until the whole class is
entangled in the hoops and all are running in the same direction together.

18   See Saw

Country: Australia
Type: Manipulative
Players: 3
Age: 10–12
Equipment: None

FIGURE 11.20   . . . begins
to fall toward . . .

Cooperative Elements: [x] Equality   [x] Trust
                         [x] Participation   [ ] Success

Teacher's Challenge: "Can you design a cooperative game with three
                       players using any available equipment? Your game
                       must stress that each player has an equal role in
                       the game, and each, in some way, must place trust
                       in the other players."

How to Play

This is a game of trust that requires close supervision. Arrange the class
into groups of three. The smallest and lightest of the three players stands
between the other two players, and keeps his body as rigid as possible.
When ready the middle player, with his eyes closed, begins to fall toward
an outside player. The outside player catches the player and gently pushes
him toward the other player. Outside players continue to move the middle
player back and forth for a few minutes.

Part Four

How to Help Children Create Their Own Games

1. Guiding Children To Create New Games
   Approach A
   Approach B
2. Guiding Children To Create New Cooperative Games

Teachers who participated in the original project that resulted in this book of international games followed set procedures when they guided children to create their own games. A detailed explanation of the steps they followed is provided in the accompanying pages to help other teachers who may wish to try this approach with their own class. Each teacher, however, should adapt or modify this procedure to cope with the needs, interests, and cultural background of the class.

1. Guiding Children to Create New Games

The procedure used in Part Two of this book, to guide children to create their own games, is called the "inventive" or "creative" games approach. It works on the basis of presenting challenges that involve the four elements of a game. The first element, shown in the accompanying chart, is the NUMBER OF PLAYERS. The second element is the PLAYING SPACE available for the game. Third is the available EQUIPMENT. And the fourth element is the SKILLS AND RULES of the game.

Creative Games Chart

Number of Players	Playing Space	Equipment	Skills and Rules
From individual activities ↓ To Partner activities ↓ To Group activities	From limited space ↓ To Use of more space	From use of simple equipment ↓ To Use of more varied and complex equipment	From single skills and rules ↓ To Use of more complex skills and rules

The four elements in the above Creative Games Chart are used as a simple grid to develop a series of challenges. However, before teachers begin to make up a series of challenges for their class, a few things should be considered. Most important is the age and background of the children. If the children are used to an exploratory way of teaching, begin with Approach A as outlined below. However, if they have been used to a fairly formal style of teaching, start with Approach B. As teachers begin to use either approach, they will adjust the type of challenge they pose on the basis of the way in which the children react to the challenges.

Approach A:

It is suggested teachers begin this approach by posing a series of simple challenges. Each successful challenge should include all four elements with a gradual increase in the number of players, playing space, pieces of equipment, and complexity of skills and rules. The next four challenges will provide a format for teachers to start using this approach. Teachers should adapt challenges to meet the needs and interests of their own class.

Situation: Twenty-eight children, age seven.
         Class sets of small equipment, such as hoops, traffic cones,
              balls, and individual ropes.
         Playing space: outdoors on blacktop area.

Challenge Number One

Give every child a utility ball and tell them to find their own space. When the children are ready, pose the following challenge:

"See if you can stay in your own space and make up a game that you can play by yourself. Your game must have a throw and a catch."

As the children are developing their own game, walk around the group and occasionally say "Remember your game must have a throw and a catch." . . ."Try to stay in your own space." . . . or other verbal cues. Also, praise children as they create ideas such as turning around in place as the ball is thrown in the air or bouncing and catching the ball.

After several minutes, ask the class to stop and sit down with their ball. Select one or two children to demonstrate their game to the class. This is an opportune time to select a child who may not have the most unique game, but nevertheless, can be given praise for his accomplishments. Move to the next challenge.

Challenge Number Two

"Can you invent a new game using your ball and hoop? At some place in your game, you must bounce the ball."

According to the Creative Games Chart, you have limited the challenge to one player, still in his own space, but now you have added new equipment and a new skill. Repeat the same procedure of walking through the group, reminding them of the elements and praising children for their creative ideas. Select a few children to demonstrate their games, then move to the next challenge.

Challenge Number Three

Refer to the Creative Games Chart. The next challenge could stay with the individual player, give her more space, and increase the number and complexity of equipment, skills, and rules. However, this example will move in the direction of increasing the number of players, so the class is arranged in partners who have one ball and two traffic cones between them. The third challenge is:

"Invent a game with your partner that will use one ball, two traffic cones, and dribbling the ball with your feet."

And the following new rule: "Player A suggests the first rule of the game then player B adds the second rule, and so on, until you have jointly planned the game."

This challenge requires children to work together in the planning and playing phases of the game. If one child is overly aggressive, she will, in most cases, plan the whole game while the less aggressive child will listen, then passively play the game. Imposing the requirement that each player take his or her turn in the planning phase, guarantees both children have a share in the creation of the game. The end result of this process is both children will enjoy the game far more than if one child dominated the planning and playing phase of the game. Follow the same procedure used previously and have one or two pairs demonstrate their game to the class.

Challenge Number Four

The next step is to present a challenge to groups of three or four children. To capitalize on the previous challenge, have the same partners join up with other partners to form groups of four. Tell the new groups of four to return two traffic cones and one ball to their containers. Limiting the equipment to one ball and two traffic cones per group of four players will challenge their collective abilities and maybe produce a game that will be a little different than the typical situation with two teams trying to throw or kick the ball through their opponent's goal. The following challenge should direct the group of four to invent a different type of game:

"See if your group of four can make up a game using one ball and two traffic cones in your own space. Your game must include passing the ball with your feet, and everyone must be moving."

This challenge is open enough to allow the group to create a game of two versus two, or a new game where each player will contribute to a single team effort. Providing only two rather than four traffic cones is also intended to encourage a group effort in whatever game is eventually created. Finally, the requirement that all players must always be moving, adds to the general complexity and fun of the game.

Once the teacher has started this process of encouraging children to create their own games, she should observe the children's behavior and make adjustments in the type of challenges, the time allowed to practice, and the way in which she encourages children to share their ideas. Generally speaking, after two or three challenges, the tone and creativity of the class will begin to emerge. From this point on use the Creative Games Chart as a grid to develop a sequence of challenges for the class.

Approach B:

Approach B is designed for older children who have been taught games through a more structured or traditional method. Games, such as poison tag, dodgeball, and marbles, are taught to children according to fixed rules and playing space. There are no variations in the game unless the teacher or the children agree upon them prior to starting the game.

FIGURE 12.1

If children have learned to play running, tag, and simple ball games through this method, an abrupt shift to asking them to create their own games may cause some initial problems. To provide a transition or bridge to this new approach, begin with a game or practice activity they know and enjoy, then gradually show them how they can change the activity to make it more challenging and enjoyable. The following example illustrates how to begin a creative games approach. With practice and success, children can be encouraged to take on more responsibility and freedom which, as you will note, is the essence of this approach.

Example: Changing the Rules of Dodgeball.

In this situation, a fourth grade teacher has organized the class into two teams to play dodgeball. The game is played for a few minutes, then the teacher asks the class to stop and listen. From the format of the Creative Games Chart, he has the following four elements through which he can introduce a change into the game.

1. Number of Players: Class is divided into two equal groups.
2. Playing Space: A large circle.
3. Skills and Rules: Throwing and hitting below the waist.
4. Equipment: Two inflated balls.

The teacher decides to pose a challenge that will vary the skills and rules. He says:

> *"When you start the next game, players in the center must keep their hands on their knees at all times, and circle players can only roll the ball."*

After a few minutes, he stops the game and tells the circle players to sit down in one corner of the gymnasium and the center players in another corner. He explains to the class that he changed the rules of their game and now is going to give them an opportunity to do the same. He says:

"Each team has thirty seconds to think up a new rule for the game."

After thirty seconds, they return to the game with the center players explaining their new rule, which usually will be a rule that applies to the circle players. Then circle players explain their rule and the game begins. After a few minutes, repeat the process, keeping the previous rules and adding the two new ones. Continue this procedure for one or more rules then shift to another game.

The process of introducing creative games has begun. The main tools are the four elements through which the teacher or children can impose limitations. This procedure should be repeated with other games, such as, Partner Tag, Crab Soccer, or Keep Away. As soon as the children feel comfortable with this approach begin to pose challenges that lead children to create their own games. The teacher's challenges in Chapter 7 will illustrate how teachers from various countries learned to pose interesting challenges to their students.

2. Guiding Children to Create New Cooperative Games

The format that is used to guide children to create their own cooperative games uses the same Creative Games Chart described in Part Two but adds one more column. To illustrate, the first four columns shown in the accompanying chart are used to set limitations for children to create their own games. Now, if we pose a challenge, such as "Make up a game with your partner, in your own space, using one ball and two hoops, and a dribble," the children may or may not create a cooperative game. Their game might become a dribbling contest around the hoops or it might become a cooperative game such as they both dribble around two hoops.

Creative Games Chart With Cooperative Elements

Game Elements				Cooperative Elements
Players	Space	Equipment	Skills and Rules	
From two to the whole class	From limited to all available space	From no equipment to many types and pieces of equipment	From no required skills and rules to many skills and specified rules	Include: equality, participation, success, and trust

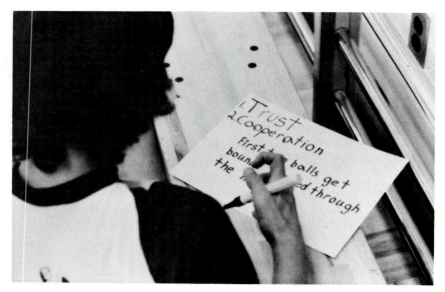

FIGURE 12.2

By adding the fifth column, COOPERATIVE ELEMENTS, we can emphasize one or more elements or cooperative behavior. These elements are described below.

Equality: Everyone has an equal role to play in the game. This means that each player "hits the ball" roughly the same number of times as any other player, "rotates" to every other position, and if part of the game requires a "leadership" role it is done on a rotating basis.

Participation: Everyone is actively involved in the game. This means that the rules of the game cannot eliminate any player from playing until the game is completed. If a player is "hit," "touched," or "misses a catch," he, in some marvelous way, continues to play.

Success: Everyone experiences success. Cooperative games have no losers! Success must also be personally defined, not something determined by a group standard.

Trust: Everyone must be able to place a measure of trust in other players. This means there are situations within the game where a player must rely on another player to "miss her," "hold her," "balance her," or perform a movement that considers her safety and well being.

It is extremely important for children to first understand the meaning of participation, trust, equality, and success, before these elements are incorporated into a cooperative game challenge. Also, there may be other elements of cooperative behavior, such as "sharing" and "fairness," that a teacher may wish to include under COOPERATIVE ELEMENTS. These elements should be discussed in class and illustrated through several cooperative games described in Part Three. As soon as the children understand these terms, pose the first cooperative games challenge described on page 128 of Part Three. If the class demonstrates they can invent a new game that stresses equality and trust, move to the next challenge or design a new challenge involving two players and one or two different elements, such as participation, success, or a new element, such as fairness. From this point on, the direction the teacher takes with her challenges will depend on the attitude of the children toward this type of game activity and, of course, their collective creative ability.

One final comment. When children are given the opportunity and accompanying freedom, they will invent very creative and enjoyable games. Keep a notepad handy and record the games you think should be saved so that other children will be able to play them as well. Like the games contained in Parts Two and Three, they will become part of an expanded games resource file for all children to play.

Bibliography

Alliance for Health, Physical Education, Recreation and Dance, *ICPHER Book of Worldwide Games and Dances,* Reston, Va., AAHPERD, 1976.

Avedon, E. M. and B. Sutton-Smith, *The Study of Games,* New York, John Wiley and Sons Inc., 1971.

Fluegelman, A., *More New Games,* New York, Doubleday and Co., Inc., 1981.

Kirchner, G., *Physical Education for Elementary School Children,* Seventh Edition, Dubuque, Wm. C. Brown Publishers, 1989.

Lucas, E. V. and E. Lucas, *Three Hundred Games and Pastimes,* Third Edition, R. Edinburgh and R. Clark Ltd., 1900.

Morris, D., *How To Change the Games that Children Play,* Minneapolis, Burgess Publishing Co., 1976.

Orlick, T., *The Cooperative Sports and Games Book,* New York, Pantheon Books, 1978.

Strutt, J., *Sports and Pastimes of the People of England,* London, Chatto and Windus, 1898.

Weinstein, M. and J. Goodman, *Playfair,* San Luis Obispo, Cal., Impact Publishers, 1980.

INDEX